Understanding Industry

Understanding Industry
Fifth Edition

Michael Barratt and Andy Mottershead
Foreword by Anita Roddick

Hodder & Stoughton

A MEMBER OF THE HODDER HEADLINE GROUP

Acknowledgements

This book is updated regularly to keep abreast of recent thinking and events. In this edition there are new case studies written in association with PricewaterhouseCoopers, The National Grid Company plc, together with a short feature linking UI with the Allied Domecq website.

Writing this book involved the help of many people at Understanding Industry, at Hodder and Stoughton and within the sponsoring companies and firms featured. We would especially like to thank Claire Hitchcock at Diageo; Sue Jillings, Diana Lynnett and Paul Molyneux at Railtrack; Bill Vestey and Chris Baker at Sony United Kingdom Limited; Marite Stragier at IBM United Kingdom Limited; Sonja Stockton and Trevor Seeley at the National Grid Company plc; David Dimmock at Standard Life Assurance Company; Colin John and Emma Reynolds at PricewaterhouseCoopers; Phil Edwards at Dixons; Charles Richardson and Layla Braithwaite at 3i Group plc; Alan George at Unilever; James Dyson at Dyson Appliances and Emma Mason from Safeway. Many thanks also to Helen Holmes at Understanding Industry, Mark Osborne at Tettenhall College and Clare Smith at Hodder and Stoughton.

Michael Barratt   Andy Mottershead

AEB assessment of Enhanced Course

In conjunction with the Understanding Industry Trust, the Associated Examining Board (AEB) has developed a test for sixth-form students following the Understanding Industry Enhanced Course, the syllabus of which is based on this book. The assessment consists of a one and a quarter-hour test containing structured, short-answer questions and is available in May annually. Schools and colleges wishing to enter candidates for the test should make their entries in the usual manner, with the AEB (tel: 01483 506506, ext. 2342).

Orders: please contact Bookpoint Ltd, 39 Milton Park, Abingdon, Oxon OX14 4TD. Telephone: (44) 01235 400414, Fax: (44) 01235 400454. Lines are open from 9.00–6.00, Monday to Saturday, with a 24 hour message answering service. Email address: orders@bookpoint.co.uk

A catalogue record for this title is available from The British Library

ISBN UI: 0 340 749 024

ISBN Hodder & Stoughton: 0 340 749 032

First published 1989 as *Understanding Industry Now*

First published by Hodder & Stoughton Educational 1994
Second edition 1996
Third edition 1997
Fourth edition 1998
Fifth edition 1999
Impression number   10 9 8 7 6 5 4 3 2
Year   2004 2003 2002 2001 2000 1999

Typeset by Wearset, Boldon, Tyne and Wear.
Printed in Great Britain for Hodder & Stoughton Educational, a division of Hodder Headline Plc, 338 Euston Road, London NW1 3BH by Redwood Books, Trowbridge, Wilts.

Contents

Logos and list of firms and organisations referred to in this book

Understanding Industry would like to thank the following companies for their generous sponsorship of the chapters of this book:

DIAGEO

Diageo

RAILTRACK

Railtrack

SONY

Sony United Kingdom Limited

IBM

IBM United Kingdom Limited

STANDARD LIFE

Standard Life Assurance Company

PriceWaterhouseCoopers ®

PricewaterhouseCoopers

Dixons

Dixons Stores Group

3i Group

Unilever

Unilever

Understanding Industry would also like to thank the following firms and organisations for their help in supplying information and/or illustrations for this publication:

3M United Kingdom Plc	J C Bamford Excavators Limited
Airdata Limited	Kodak Limited
Allied Domecq plc	Levi Strauss (UK) Limited
Apple Computer UK Ltd	Marks & Spencer Plc
Birds Eye Wall's	Messier Dowty
The Body Shop International Plc	Mitsubishi Electric Europe (B.V.)
Braebourne Ltd	The National Grid Company plc
Chartered Institute of Marketing	Racal Electronics Group
Clarks International	Renishaw Plc
The Denby Pottery Company Ltd	Rolls Royce Plc
Department of Trade and Industry	Rover Group Ltd
Dyson Appliances Ltd	Safeway Plc
Ford Motor Company Limited	SmithKline Beecham
GEC Alsthom	Tesco Stores Ltd
Glaxo Pharmaceuticals UK Limited	Texas Instruments
Grand Metropolitan Plc	Vauxhall Motors Limited
Hewlett-Packard Limited	Virgin Management Limited
Imperial Chemicals Industries Plc	Volvo Car UK Limited

Preface

DAVID MILLAR

This year is the 21st Anniversary of Understanding Industry. 21 years of informing, involving and inspiring young people.

Young people need practical information about the World of Work. Could there be a better way of doing this than having people who actually do the job to tell students about it. At Understanding Industry we call the volunteer managers 'Session Leaders' – they are actually role models.

Traditionally, most young people gleaned information about the World of Work from friends rather than from teachers or from other professionals. It might have worked in the past when skill levels were lower and we had a full employment economy. However, in an increasingly competitive world, against a background of rapidly changing technology and globalisation, it simply is not good enough.

Too often, the choices our young people make are negative. They don't want to do this or they don't want to do that. What UI does is to turn this around – the choices they make are positive.

David Millar
Chief Executive
Understanding Industry

ABOUT UNDERSTANDING INDUSTRY

Understanding Industry (UI) is an educational charity which works to increase knowledge of, and improve attitudes towards, industry and commerce through the delivery of high quality programmes designed to inform, involve and inspire 16–19 year-old students and to enhance their key skills. Over 1,500 companies from industry and commerce support the work of UI.

UI is unique because it provides a first-hand view, in the classroom, of the world of industry and commerce. Each session on a UI course is led by a working business manager and incorporates the most up-to-date business practice. The sessions are participative in style, involving exercises, case studies and business games. This book, *Understanding Industry*, is designed to cover the main areas of industry and commerce which can be included in the UI course: Marketing and sales, Design and development, Information technology, Production, Personnel, Finance, Management, Growing businesses and Integration. Courses are tailored to the particular needs and interests of the individual school or college, either as part of a general studies programme or as a support for examined subjects.

For more information about UI and its work please contact:

Understanding Industry
Enterprise House
59–65 Upper Ground
London SE1 9PQ
Tel: 0171 620 0735

Foreword

ANITA RODDICK

You are about to enter a world of opportunity unlike that of your parents. Although there are no jobs for life, there are new jobs requiring new thinking and new talents. That's where you come in. And that's where this book will help you consider your first steps.

The world of business can seem a daunting place for people still in education. You will be wondering just how relevant are your skills and qualifications for the world that awaits you. As you step out on a 40-year journey, however, if you are ready to embrace the unknown, you will meet a world more than ready to give you responsibility and reward.

Industry means being active. You may find that you are being asked to run before you can walk. That is the fast pace of modern business. Your ability to grasp opportunities and shoulder responsibilities will depend on how quickly you can absorb the language of business.

In this book you will find words like 'R&D', 'differentiation', 'profit sharing' and 'quality management' – all words that have held meaning for many years in business. But technology is introducing words and concepts whose implications are as yet unclear and will depend upon new thinking. Business and industry are changing. The world is calling out for new ways of doing business. Today, companies are barely getting used to environmental management. Tomorrow, they will find themselves required to deal with social issues like never before.

Companies like The Body Shop depend on young people to come in and take on these challenges with energy and commitment. The era of the 9–5 job for an easy pay cheque is long gone. There is a new tension between employer and employee. A company in the age of globalisation makes more demands on more employees. An employee working for such a company demands rewards which go beyond the financial.

We are moving into a time when companies are so tied to the communities in which they operate, that a new generation of people entering the workplace will wonder how business ever acted as if only shareholders mattered.

As you read this book, I would ask you to reflect on the fact that when you leave school, that is the beginning of your education. I'm still learning and the business world never ceases to amaze me, though I spend most of my time trying to change it. But that's my attitude towards the world of work. What's yours? Whatever it is, I wish you good luck on your journey.

Anita Roddick
Founder, The Body Shop

Introduction

IN ASSOCIATION WITH

DIAGEO

Wealth creation

Business is the process of making a profit by providing products or services which people want to buy. As a result of the drive to make a profit, firms create wealth which is then distributed within the economy. For example, Denby Pottery creates wealth by transforming raw Derbyshire clay into cups, saucers and other tableware bought throughout the world. In the process, 700 staff are employed directly, many others are employed indirectly (suppliers and distributors, for instance) and local and national government receive over $£2$ million a year in taxes.

The more initiative, invention and care taken by Denby staff, the more products they can sell and the more customers are prepared to pay for the Denby name. So, design and development, marketing, people and production are all key factors in wealth creation.

Statistics show that nearly 18 per cent of all the tax collected in Britain is from employers. That proportion is lower than in countries such as Japan and Germany, yet still represents a huge contribution towards government spending on such things as hospitals, roads, schools and old age pensions. So,

business does not only create wealth for shareholders, it also helps to provide the jobs and the public services we all rely on.

Every person involved in the success of a business can be referred to as a **stakeholder**. Such a term was made famous by Tony Blair and his reference to the 'stakeholder economy' – by this he meant that every person and every institution should be able to share in the success of the economy. In a similar way, the success of an individual business can be shared amongst the stakeholders of that business.

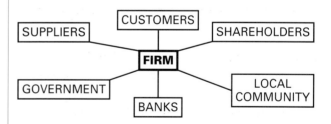

Figure 1.1

* * *

Over recent years, four factors stand out in their impact upon the economic environment for British businesses:

● Wide swings between boom and recession.
● The arrival of Japanese companies and management ideas.

- A structural change towards service businesses.
- A shift towards flexible labour markets, partly through privatization.

Economic background

___

A review of our recent economic and business past shows that in 1899, Britain sold one in three of the world's exports of manufactured goods. She was the world's most important exporter by far. By the late 1970s Britain's share had fallen to 7.5 per cent, dwarfed by Germany, America and Japan. In fact, with only 1.5 per cent of the world's population, Britain's export performance was still quite impressive, but there was concern about her relative decline.

Partly as a response to this, the Conservative government of 1979 swept to power with a determination to revitalise the economy by:

- Lowering income taxes to restore people's incentive to work.
- Cutting inflation through tight monetary policy.
- Creating tough new laws to curb the power of trade unions.
- Establishing an 'enterprise culture' through **privatization** and deregulation.

The overall approach was to reduce the role of government to give managers the right and the power to manage. Then people could be expected to set up their own businesses and to take pride in running them profitably.

The effect of these policies was dramatic. 1980 saw the sharpest recession for half a century as firms struggled to cope with high interest rates and exchange rates caused by the attempt to cut inflation. By the mid-1980s, however, a major recovery was underway. The rate of new business start-ups rose dramatically, as did the level of inward investment. American companies such as IBM and Motorola were joined by Japanese giants such as

Mitsubishi, Nissan and Toyota. All were keen to set up factories in Britain – a member of the European Union with a government establishing favourable conditions for employers.

Despite a dramatic collapse in the stock market in October 1987, the economy kept moving ahead strongly. The government was convinced its policies had transformed the economic potential of the country, enabling it to grow faster than ever before. In the March 1988 Budget, the Chancellor of the Exchequer cut taxes for those in higher-earning brackets, to encourage enterprise still further.

Yet this proved a step too far. The tax cuts led to extra consumer spending, stoking up the already buoyant demand for imported goods and property. Rapid rises in house prices added to inflation, while the high level of imports pushed the balance between exports and imports severely into the red. In an attempt to control these excesses, interest rates were pushed up sharply, doubling between spring and autumn 1988.

Economies change course very slowly, so the effects only showed through in mid-1990. There was a fall in the demand for goods bought on credit, such as houses and cars. Firms cut back on investment and staffing, as they struggled to pay the high interest charges on their loans. The period between 1990 and 1993 proved the longest recession of the century, with economic output falling slowly but steadily, month after month. Many house owners who had purchased their properties in the mid-eighties, now found they were saddled with the problem of negative equity (having a mortgage at a higher level than the market value of the house).

Recovery came when Britain's withdrawal from the European Exchange Rate Mechanism (ERM) allowed the pound to fall by 15 per cent against all foreign currencies. This made British firms 15 per cent more competitive at a stroke. New export opportunities opened up, first in America and then in Europe.

Rising production for export started to lead Britain out of recession during 1993. Scarred by the recession, consumer and business confidence recovered very slowly, but by late 1994 an upward path was established.

The structure of industry

——

Britain has a mixed economy, which means that some firms operate in the private sector whilst others are under direct state control, these being the nationalised industries. Many of these have been privatized in recent years, such as BT and British Gas. There are four sectors within the economy:

- The **primary** sector – where resources are extracted from the ground, e.g. mining, quarrying, drilling for oil, farming and fishing.
- The **secondary** sector – where these primary products or raw materials are used to manufacture goods, e.g. electronics, steel, cars, clothes etc.
- The **tertiary** sector – where services are provided, e.g. banking, retailing, advertising, tourism and so on, and also public services such as health, education, defence etc.
- The **quaternary** sector – where services are provided using IT (information technology).

Businesses in the private sector vary in size from small start-up firms to large multinational corporations. Yet, despite this diversity there are only

TABLE I.I *Types of business unit*

	Sole traders	*Partnership*	*Limited company*
Owners	One owner	Two to 20 owners – can be more in partnerships of solicitors and accountants etc.	Minimum of two shareholders
Management decisions	Owner	Partners	Board of directors elected by shareholders
Provision of funds	Owner's funds	Partners' funds contributed in amounts laid down in partnership agreement	Share capital up to maximum amount stated in memorandum – for public limited company the minimum to be **quoted** on the Stock Exchange is £50,000
Financial risk	Owner has unlimited liability	Partners have unlimited liability	Liability is limited to value of shareholding
Allocation of profits	Owner takes profits	Partners agree on how profit should be paid	Directors decide how much profit should be paid as dividends on shares and how much is ploughed back as investment
Duration	Ends on death of owner	Can be dissolved according to terms stated in partnership agreement, or ends on death of partner	Ends on liquidation, when assets are sold off and the company is legally wound up

three different legal forms of business: sole trader, partnership and limited company.

Most entrepreneurs operate as sole traders initially. This is the easiest way to start up, as no complicated legal formalities are involved. By definition, entrepreneurs are undertaking a risk in a new commercial venture. They have unlimited liability, which means that if the business fails, they may have to sell their home and personal possessions to pay outstanding bills. This is balanced by the fact that they keep any profits made and have complete freedom in decision making.

In time, sole traders may decide to form a partnership – a decision that is usually taken in order to raise more capital for expansion. In order to avoid disagreements, most partners draw up a formal partnership agreement. This includes details on, for instance, how much capital is contributed by each partner and the ratio in which profits and losses are to be shared.

As the business develops, further capital for expansion can be obtained by becoming a company and selling shares. Shares in private limited companies are not freely available to the general public and can only be transferred with the agreement of the directors. Shares in public limited companies, on the other hand, can be sold to the general public. Companies must have share capital of at least £50,000 before they can 'go public'. Only public companies are able to have their shares floated on the Stock Exchange.

In becoming a company the business acquires a legal identity which is separate from the shareholders. This means that it can be sued. Shareholders also have limited liability; if the business fails they are only responsible for an amount equivalent to their original investment. Therefore, anyone owed money by a company that goes into liquidation may never receive a penny. For this reason, a private limited company must have **Ltd** after its name and a public company **Plc** after its name. This makes it clear to suppliers or anyone else dealing with them, that their liability is limited. Every company must also place a copy of its accounts at Companies House, so that anyone can check whether the firm is financially sound.

The essential differences between these three types of business units are shown in Table 1.1.

Does manufacturing still matter?

Today, three quarters of those in work are engaged in the service sector. **Private sector** jobs in retailing, finance, and leisure and tourism are added to by **public sector** work in health and social care, education and the civil service. As the number of people employed in manufacturing fell during the 1980s, it became fashionable to believe that Britain's future rested with service industries. Table 1.2 shows how such a view could take hold. The only two categories showing job growth are services and the self-employed (most of whom provide services in any case). Nowadays, fewer than one fifth of jobs are in manufacturing.

Employment opportunities within the primary and secondary sectors have been declining steadily over the last twenty years as a consequence of automation, foreign competition and the government of the day. For every 10 people living in the UK, four work to support all 10. Of those that work, there are three employed in the service sector and only one employed within manufacturing! Table 1.2 clearly shows the changing pattern of employment.

So can the country afford to let manufacturing wither and die? Some people would say yes, believing that Britain can prosper solely by selling services to the world. They argue that services can create wealth as well as, if not better than, manufacturing. They point to Britain's huge overseas earnings from tourism, financial services, education, royalties and patents. Others disagree.

TABLE 1.2 *Changes in the number of jobs by sector 1979–96*

	1979 (000s)	1996 (000s)	Change (000s)	Percentage change
Primary sector	705	279.9	425.1	−60.3
Secondary sector:				
All production	8,642	4,982.3	3,659.7	−42.3
Of which:				
Manufacturing	7,073	3,944.7	3,128.3	−44.2
Services	13,240	16,176	2,936	+22.2
ALL EMPLOYEES	22,587	21,438.3	1,148.7	−5
Self-employed*	1,842	3,500*	1,658	+90
TOTAL WORKFORCE IN EMPLOYMENT	24,429	24,938.3	509.3	−2.1

Source: *HMSO Annual Abstract of Statistics and Labour Market Trends*, November 1996
*estimated

The founder and honorary chairman of Sony, Akio Morita, has warned that 'in the long run an economy that has lost its manufacturing base has lost its vital centre. A service-based economy has no engine to drive it'. He goes on to add, 'When manufacturing prospers, all industries connected with it prosper – not only are more components, parts and salesmen needed, but more accountants, more dentists, more petrol stations, more supermarkets and more schools. Service industries cannot flourish in isolation – they depend on manufacturing to support them.'

Manufacturing industries, in turn, rely on a network of service industries within the key areas of banking and finance, law, distribution and marketing. Clearly, manufacturing and the service sector are dependent on each other. Consumer spending in developed economies tends to shift towards services such as transport and tourism, but manufacturing remains important.

In which areas does Britain have a competitive advantage?

In *The Competitive Advantage of Nations*, Michael Porter compares the industrial nations of the world in order to identify their competitive strengths and weaknesses. In Britain's case, he identifies a range of areas where a strong national competitive position has been achieved.

The largest concentrations of British competitive advantage are in packaged goods (including food, alcoholic drinks and household products) and consumer goods retailing. Another important cluster is in financial or financially-related services such as insurance, trading and money management. Significant clusters are also present in pharmaceuticals, chemicals, computing equipment and software, entertainment and leisure products, defence and clothing.

It is encouraging for Britain's future prosperity that so many of these industries with a strong competitive position are in the fast growing 'sunrise' industries rather than the declining 'sunset' industries, such as metalworking and shipbuilding. Britain's successful sunrise industries include motor vehicles, electronics, aerospace, pharmaceuticals and consumer goods in general.

BRITISH BUSINESSES WITH INTERNATIONAL STRENGTH

Consumer products
- food and drink
- clothing
- household goods
- pharmaceuticals

Industrial products
- chemicals
- cars
- electronics
- aerospace

Services
- retailing
- insurance
- banking
- leisure and tourism

Many of the sunrise industries also have the important advantage of being knowledge- rather than labour-intensive. According to Professor Douglas McWilliams, the former chief economic adviser at the Confederation of British Industry (CBI), 'Low-skilled production is increasingly migrating to developing economies with rock-bottom labour costs, particularly those around the Pacific Rim. The only way we can remain competitive is by constantly up-skilling the manufacturing base. Companies must make themselves more innovative and high tech in order to compensate for the jobs that will inevitably disappear overseas.' In other words, those firms that do remain labour-intensive are likely to face an uncertain future.

What is the key to greater competitiveness?

Competing on a world-beating scale involves being successful in a number of key areas. The first step is to develop a strong consumer focus. This means listening to what customers want in order to respond to, or anticipate their needs. Then to develop and introduce innovative new products in order to stay ahead of the competition. This requires a large scale commitment of funds for research and development.

In addition, the selective use of automation can be beneficial, though large scale automation is not appropriate to all firms and all industries. There is a danger that if the production processes are not streamlined beforehand, automation will merely speed up the existing problems, not solve them. Nevertheless, automation can, if it is well planned, increase the rate of production and improve reliability.

However, the costs of developing innovative new products and of automating are so great that there may be a long period before the investment yields a profit. It is vital to the long-term competitiveness of industry that firms invest in the future, so City financiers must be prepared to lend 'patient money'. Unlike their Japanese and German counterparts, they have tended to be preoccupied with short-term profits at the expense of long-term investment.

WHAT ARE THE REQUIREMENTS FOR COMPETING IN A GLOBAL MARKET?

- a competitive price
- good quality
- reliability
- prompt delivery
- innovative design
- after-sales service
- flexibility

British firms would certainly be vulnerable if they attempted to compete in world markets by virtue of low prices alone. No less important are the quality of design and manufacture and the standards of customer service.

Competitiveness today depends on much more than low prices. It relies on a whole range of non-price factors, including good design, technological innovation, reliability, on-time delivery and after-sales service; in short, on quality. Firms such as Rover and Cadbury Schweppes have managed to transform their fortunes in recent years through their success in getting all these aspects of quality right.

This does not mean, however, that they can now afford to sit back. The targets for world-class manufacturing are constantly expanding. As ever, it appears that the Japanese are setting the standards to beat. Simon Caulkin points out in an article in *Management Today* that, 'Already the Japanese are beginning to talk of "taken for granted" quality and product features, and are moving on to compete by "surprising" and "delighting" customers . . . quality and customer satisfaction are 1980's concepts. The aim now must be not just to meet customer needs but to exceed them.'

Flexible employees

Traditionally, British workplaces were organised in a rigid fashion. Employees were hired and trained to do one task and unless they were promoted might receive no further training. Tight **demarcation** lines showed where one job ended and the next one began. All that was expected of an employee was to work effectively at the task set out by the boss. Very few would feel involved enough to suggest ideas for improvements, nor did the employers expect this.

This rigid, narrow focus of work was also sought by trade unions. Employees working on single tasks maximised job numbers and therefore job security. Rigid job demarcation served the interests of employers, workers and trade unions equally.

Comparably rigid systems covered:

- Wage bargaining, with trade unions negotiating with employers on behalf of all employees (**collective bargaining**).
- Pay scales, with every employee on the same job grade receiving the same rate of pay.
- Terms and conditions of employment, with nearly all staff on full-time, permanent work status.

The 1980s and 1990s have seen dramatic changes towards greater flexibility. Japanese firms brought new employment practices to Britain, insisting that employees learn the skills to perform a wide variety of jobs. Multi-skilling replaced demarcation. The role of trade unions was also changed as many of the new firms demanded no-strike deals.

Also important has been high unemployment. Staff anxious to keep their jobs have proved willing to accept many changes in their conditions and terms at work. Firms have been able to reduce their numbers of full-time employees and top up their workforce with temporary or part-time staff as and when necessary for seasonal or other reasons.

Privatization has also been a factor. First came the sale of the state-owned **nationalised** industries such as British Telecom, British Gas and British Steel. Shares in these giant businesses were sold to private investors through the stock exchange. Less public, but perhaps more important, was the move to contract out services to the private sector. Councils found private contractors to sweep the streets or run their accounts departments.

In both cases, the effects were similar. Strongly unionised public sector organisations switched to the private sector. Often, unions were no longer recognised by the private sector contractors, so employers found it easier to change working practices and terms of employment. The trend to flexibility was given a boost, sparking off similar actions by large private sector firms, contracting out services such as cleaning, security and deliveries.

From the employer's point of view, the job market of recent years has become favourable. In his book, *The Age of Unreason*, Charles Handy cites several marked changes in the structural make-up of the workforce over recent years. The key characteristics of these changes have been:

- The move from full-time to part-time workforce.
- More women joining the labour force than ever before.
- The move from permanent to temporary, renewable contracts.
- An increasing amount of work which is subcontracted out to other specialised companies, e.g. catering, cleaning and computer services.

This has resulted in what Handy calls the Shamrock organisation where the three leaves of the shamrock represent:
- The core workforce.
- The contractual fringe.
- The flexible labour force.

He believes that this will continue into the future, with job security only existing for the vital, highly educated, core workforce.

CASE STUDY

Diageo – the skills required for business success*

What factors have high achievers such as Richard Branson (Virgin), Anita Roddick (Body Shop) and Sir Ian MacLaurin (Tesco) in common? Is it their exam achievements? Their social contacts? Their inherited wealth? Or do they share some personal

*The name of the company formed from the merger of Guinness Plc and Grand Metropolitan Plc in late 1997.

qualities that have been important in their successful business careers? Without question it is the latter; qualities that can benefit anyone starting out in business.

Diageo has looked hard at defining the key personal qualities and how best to develop them. An analysis of the company's own managers has shown that success depends upon:

1 Commitment (to results, to quality, to excellence and to change).
2 Leadership (directing, motivating, inspiring and building cooperation).
3 Personal skills (confidence, maturity, communicating and influencing).
4 People development (counselling and developing others; reflecting on own strengths and weaknesses).
5 Problem solving (gets to the heart of issues; numerate; creative; good judgement; willing to take risks).
6 Strategic thinking (thinks about the whole business, about trends and about the future; copes with change).

Most of these qualities can be developed outside the classroom as well as within it. The captain of a school/college team will need to develop all the first four qualities to be really effective. Within the classroom, there should also be many opportunities to learn these personal qualities – whether through case studies, classroom presentations, project work or role plays.

Diageo identifies and develops these skills by setting demanding tasks for young high-flyers. In the past, university students were recruited for places on a two year management trainee course. Now the company favours a less formal 'business course'. The high achievers on this course may be hired for six months and given a project to complete. If this goes well and both sides like what they see, a management post will be offered. The benefits of this are its flexibility and the fact that it tests people's ability at work rather than at study.

In 1996 20-year-old Pasi Lankinen, from Finland, was selected for the programme. He was set the task of devising a new 'knowledge programme' for the United Distillers sales force. The problem was that United

Distillers sells so many different products (well over 1,000!) that new sales staff found it impossible to learn quickly about the traditions, the product qualities and the target customer for all the brands. This would make it impossible to sell effectively. So Pasi was set the important task of improving the existing training programme.

At the outset, Pasi assumed his task would be largely academic: interviewing, researching and writing. After reading everything he could about the whiskies, gins, brandies, liqueurs and many other alcoholic drinks made by United Distillers, Pasi had to start talking to the relevant sales and product managers. What were their needs?

To his surprise, Pasi found that he had to do much more than just phone up for appointments. Even though he was working on a task that would help the whole business and for a senior Head Office manager, almost everyone seemed too busy to see him. Only after careful discussions with, and coaching from, management development professionals was he able to see things from other managers' points of view. They had deadlines and targets to meet. Why should they spend time on something with no short-term payback run by a 20-year-old, fresh from college?

He learnt that he needed to *sell* his project to them before they would be helpful. This required a clear understanding of their goals and needs, careful planning and also a degree of assertiveness. He also learnt, the hard way, that he needed to be flexible about his style of approach. In Britain he could be quite informal, addressing managers by their first names. When he visited the Spanish subsidiary, however, using first names was regarded as disrespectful, even offensive.

Pasi also followed up his contacts by socialising after work and by keeping in touch by phone or in person. This was crucial because not only might he need to return for more information, but also these same people would be vital – later on – to the successful implementation of the new programme. As he came to know the staff better, he learnt who were the people who could 'get things done' (not necessarily because of their position) and which 'strings to pull'. In the terms of the six categories set out at the start,

Pasi's experience pointed to the crucial role of categories one, three and four: commitment, personal skills and self-development.

Managing people effectively requires skills of persuasion and communication. You can achieve some things by telling staff what to do, but getting the best out of people requires everyone to believe in what is being done. A Diageo subsidiary overseas underwent ferocious streamlining in order to meet an ambitious profit target. Although the target was met, much hard work was needed to sustain morale and to keep the commitment of the best people. The key managerial skills required were communication, motivation and the ability to build relationships.

And Pasi? He has returned to university to finish his degree, but left behind a well constructed slide presentation showing his recommendations for the new knowledge programme. He regarded the whole exercise as 'the most challenging thing I have ever done' and wants to return to the company once his degree is over. Diageo regards that as a compliment indeed.

ACTIVITY

How well do you perform against the Diageo criteria? What evidence is there that you have these qualities? What might you do to fill any gaps?

QUALITIES	EVIDENCE
1 Commitment (to results, to quality, to excellence).	Exam results......... Other............
2 Leadership (directing, motivating, inspiring).	Captain/leader........ Other............
3 Personal skills (confidence, maturity, communicating).	Telephone manner...... Influencing others......
4 Development (of others; and reflecting on own performance).	Trained others........ Self-knowledge.......
5 Problem solving (analytic; numerate; risk-taker; creative)	Analytic/numerate...... Risk-taking.........

6 Strategic (thinks of whole   Clear goals . . . .

business, trends and future).   Plan for achieving them . .

The more evidence you have of fulfilling requirements such as these, the better. Can you think of ways to fill any of the gaps?

Japanese firms in Britain – competitor or regenerator?

The first major Japanese company to establish a plant in the UK was YKK, the zip manufacturer, in 1971. This was followed in 1974 by the Sony television factory in South Wales. The trend continued in the 1970s, but accelerated in the 1980s as it seemed likely that moves to closer economic union within Europe might shut out Japanese exports. Japanese firms now employ over 30,000 British workers, mainly in areas of traditionally high unemployment, such as South Wales and the North East. Britain has been the most successful European country at bringing Japanese investment into new factories and financial services.

So why is Britain proving so attractive to Japanese companies?

● Due to the importance of the American market, English is the first foreign language taught in Japan.
● British wage rates for factory workers are the lowest among the developed European countries.
● Non-wage costs are much lower for employers in Britain than elsewhere; in France, employers pay taxes that add more than a quarter to their wage bill.

● The attitude of successive British governments has been very welcoming to the Japanese; elsewhere there was mistrust of the motives and methods of Japanese firms.
● The industrial relations climate is seen as highly favourable; British unions have been willing to sign single-union, no-strike deals with Japanese firms.
● The success in Britain of the early pioneers such as Sony ensured that other Japanese firms felt happy to follow.

From the 1970s, there has been a fear that the Japanese would provide little of long-term benefit to the British economy. The concern was that Japanese factories in Britain would be 'screwdriver plants', merely assembling imported components. This would provide semi-skilled jobs, but not the professional tasks such as Research and Development (R & D), product design and production engineering.

Today firms such as Canon, Nissan and Sony have looked for more from their British employees. They have set up R & D operations here to boost the quality of their investment – away from assembly into high value-added activities. There has also been a beneficial spin-off from Japanese techniques for managing people and production. The success of Japanese managers at achieving high productivity with British workers has forced a rethink about management practices in this country.

In addition, most Japanese companies are committed to increasing the amount of components they buy from Britain. The Sony plant at Bridgend, for instance, now obtains over 90 per cent of its components locally. Typically, when Japanese firms first arrive they find it hard to obtain local supplies of the right quality and reliability. Yet within a year or two they build close relationships with small numbers of local producers whose competitiveness is boosted permanently from the work put into meeting the demands of the Japanese buyers.

Marketing and sales

IN ASSOCIATION WITH

RAILTRACK

Introduction: what is marketing?

Firms do not have a choice about whether or not to carry out any marketing. Every organisation markets itself, if only through the kinds of products and services it offers and the standard of its customer service. The only choice is between whether the marketing is done haphazardly or whether it is done systematically, through coordinating every aspect of the **marketing effort**. Marketing is often confused with selling or advertising. While both of these functions are involved, the total marketing effort also includes assessing customer needs and carrying out market research, together with the development of the product and its pricing, promotion and distribution.

The key task for any business is to get its marketing right, but this also means the company must be good at everything else from research and development to manufacturing and from quality control to financial control. Marketing does not function in isolation from other departments, but permeates the company. It is no more the exclusive responsibility of the marketing

department than profitability is solely the responsibility of the finance department.

According to the Chartered Institute of Marketing, it is 'the management process responsible for identifying, anticipating and satisfying customer requirements profitably'. This means getting the right product or service in the right place at the right time, in the right quantities and at the right price, to ensure enough profit for the company.

WHY HAS MARKETING INCREASED?

In the early days of industrialisation, output could not keep pace with demand. Industries therefore operated in a **sellers' market**. This resulted in a **production orientation**, where firms concentrated on producing the goods they wanted to make. The disregard for consumer preferences at the time is summed up by the 'take it or leave it' attitude of Henry Ford. His comment, 'They can have any colour they like, as long as it's black', reveals an offhand approach which can largely be explained by the lack of competition – Ford had a 50 per cent share of the American car market in the 1920s.

However, particularly since the Second World War, firms have had to adopt a **marketing orientation**, in order to survive in today's fiercely competitive markets. Most industries now operate in a **buyers' market**, where consumers can choose what they want to buy from the immense variety of products and services on offer. Firms have to concentrate on producing the goods the market wants, rather than the ones they happen to make.

This changing orientation applies also to overseas markets. Firms can no longer presume, in these days of global competition, that the world will beat a path to their door. Competition has intensified as the open market in Europe presents a tremendous marketing opportunity, but also poses a huge potential threat for the unprepared firm.

What do people need and want?

Marketing starts with finding out what motivates customers to buy a particular product or service. As Peter Drucker, the American management expert, emphasises, 'The aim of marketing is to make selling superfluous. The aim is to know and understand the customer so well that the product or service sells itself.'

 This means identifying the customer's **needs** and **wants**. Philip Kotler, in his book, *Principles of Marketing*, defines a need as 'a state of felt deprivation in a person' while wants are 'needs as shaped by our culture and personality'. In other words, all people need to eat, but one person may want beefburger and chips while another might want salmon and caviar. Wants only become **demand** when people have the resources to acquire what they want. For example, many people might want a Rolls Royce but only a few can afford to buy one, so the demand for Rolls Royces is small.

American psychologist AH Maslow has argued that people have different levels of needs. They seek to satisfy lower level needs, such as those for food, drink, shelter and safety, before trying to fulfil their higher order needs, for things such as social

acceptance, status and self-fulfilment. However, people do respond differently in the way they satisfy a particular need according to their attitudes, social values and so on. The implication, therefore, is that consumers do not simply buy a product or service – they buy *solutions* to their perceived problems or needs. If the marketing effort is to be successful, it must emphasise the *benefits* consumers will gain by using the product or service.

Maslow's hierarchy of needs

In fact, what people want is usually far more than they need. In buying an expensive house, the successful person is making a statement about his or her status and position in society rather than just buying a shelter from the elements. Which marketing campaign for expensive houses is likely to be most effective – one which emphasises how structurally sound the houses are, or one which portrays a comfortable lifestyle with glamorous people in elegant room settings? In the same way most campaigns are cleverly aimed at subtly exploiting the often subconscious wants which influence people's buying decisions.

As most consumers' needs and wants are already being catered for, much effort also goes into creating new needs and wants by developing innovative products. Once introduced onto the market, these exploit wants which were **latent** and not expressed until the new product became available. How many people knew they wanted a personal stereo until Sony actually brought out their Walkman™?

Innovative products can therefore stimulate new consumer wants, but what about the reverse situation? Can new consumer wants stimulate innovative products being developed? In fact, this has already happened. For instance, in the plastics and synthetic fibre industries, the marketing people tell the researchers what properties they need and the researchers then design those materials. The implications of the fact that we can now 'innovate to order' are far reaching.

 DISCUSSION POINTS

1 *Do advertisers encourage materialism by constantly exploiting people's needs and wants?*

2 *What are some of the products and services which are advertised to exploit each level of Maslow's hierarchy of needs?*

Is market research essential?

Carrying out detailed market research, whether it concerns products and services aimed at domestic consumers or those aimed at industrial consumers, is the first step in any effective marketing campaign. Market research provides information which is sufficiently objective to form a basis for decision making. Firms generally start by looking at the information already available within their own company, from sales and account records and so on. These can show:

● Which products are most profitable.
● Whether sales fall into a pattern by type of product, by customer, by geographical area or by size of order.

● Whether the company is becoming too dependent on a few customers or products.
● Which customer accounts are most profitable.
● What proportion of sales quotations result in actual orders.

The next step for firms is to consult other sources of information which have already been published, such as government publications, media reports, newspapers and journals. These can show:

● Whether the total market for a particular product or service is growing, static or declining.
● What changes are taking place in the market.
● Who the main competitors are.

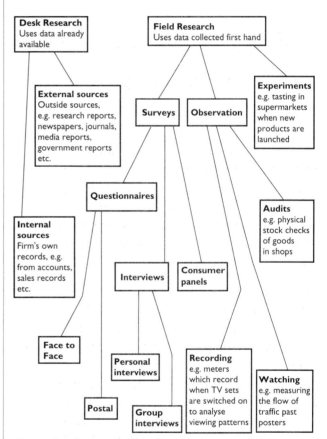

Quantitative methods of market research

If neither of these forms of **desk research** provides all the information required, the firm may then decide some **field research** is needed, which it can either do itself or commission a market research agency to carry out.

In any case, only a sample of people would be researched. It is not practical or even necessary to contact every person in the potential market! The group of people can be a random sample picked from the electoral registers, telephone directories and so on, or a stratified sample, where a representative cross-section of the population in terms of factors such as age, sex, income etc. is researched. Alternatively, interviewers may be given a quota. If they are conducting street interviews this means that they can choose whom to interview, providing they survey a certain number of people from, for example, each age group.

Once the size and type of sample has been chosen, firms can then carry out **quantitative research** to provide answers to such questions as *how many* people buy their product. They can also carry out **qualitative research** by means of group discussions and in-depth interviews, to establish such factors as *who* buys their products and *why*.

Market research cannot, of course, eliminate business risk, but it can greatly reduce the guesswork element.

STAGES OF MARKET RESEARCH

● *Decide on purpose of market research, what information needs to be obtained and what action will be taken as a result of research findings* ✔ ☐

● *Decide on most appropriate market research method(s) taking into account time and budget constraints* ☐

● *Decide on size and composition of sample to be studied, in line with the objectives of the research* ☐

● *Carry out research using appropriate methods* ☐

● *Gather and analyse data from research* ☐

● *Present findings in a report. Summarise main findings, draw conclusions and make recommendations on what actions need to be taken as a result of research* ☐

Stages of market research

Potentially disastrous situations can thus be avoided, such as when a huge capital investment is made in a product for which there is no demand. This sounds unlikely, yet even highly innovative products have been known to fail because they are sold in a market which has not been correctly identified.

CASE STUDY

The Solero success story

Most new products hit the marketplace in a blaze of advertising and publicity. Wall's Solero was different. It arrived in retail freezer cabinets in June 1994 almost unannounced. Yet by August it was the UK's third fastest selling hand-held ice cream. Wall's were delighted by its success and decided that in 1995 it would be launched throughout Europe and supported by a £3 million marketing budget in the UK.

The Solero story started with a marketing decision to tackle the adult refreshment sector of the ice-cream market. The goal was to repeat the success of Magnum in the indulgence sector. Birds Eye Wall's dominated the market for impulse-purchase ice cream, so a product was needed that could stimulate total market growth by attracting new users. Research indicated that an opportunity existed for a premium quality product targeting 20–35-year-olds, which offered both refreshment and indulgence. As the brand mapping diagram on page 15 shows, Solero was to open up a new segment of the market.

An initial meeting was arranged in March 1993 to bring together product development, marketing and production staff. After their discussions, a product developer said, 'While you're all here, what do you think of this?' They were given a square, orange-coloured lolly on a stick. A couple of licks of the exotic fruit coating, and the discovery of dairy ice cream inside, convinced them that the right product had been found before they had even started looking. A target launch date was set for Spring 1995.

The development team explained that the smoothness of the fruit ice required a new, patentable production technique. Patents were immediately pursued and the implications for factory layout were examined.

The product's shape, taste and size were refined during the summer, using qualitative research. The whole product concept was then researched in Germany, Italy, Holland and Portugal in November 1993, to see how well it might perform as a Europe-wide brand. The results were so encouraging that the Birds Eye Wall's Board decided to rush the project forward for a 1994 test launch in Britain.

Meanwhile an appropriate brand name was sought that could be pronounced and registered throughout Europe. A specialist brand name agency found that only 42 from a 'shortlist' of 950 names could pass both tests. And the brand team liked none of them. Further work produced a final choice between two: Oasis and Solero. The Solero name was not available in Belgium, but its association with the sun and its exceptional pronounceability made it the winner. (In Belgium, you will have to ask for Soledo.)

At the same time, the packaging design had been decided upon and the price set at 80p – between Opal Fruits at 65p and Magnum at 90p. The product was ready for launch.

As June 1994 approached it was still not certain whether the factory would be able to produce this new style of ice cream in sufficient numbers. So it was decided that no advertising would be run until it was clear that production could keep up with demand. This was fortunate, because although factory output proved buoyant, an exceptionally hot July sent demand rocketing for all refreshment products.

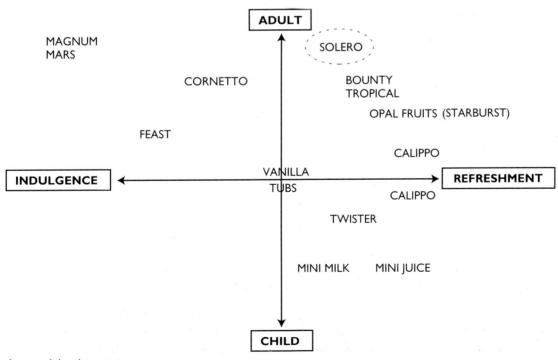

Impulse positioning map

Table 2.1 *SOLERO: Volume share of total adult refreshment market (annual totals)*

YEAR	SOLERO	SPLIT	OPAL FRUITS (STARBURST)
1995	25.1	13.2	14.7
1996	39.8	12.3	12.7
1997	51.6	11.8	12.9

The table shows Solero's rise in market share over the product's life. Pleasingly for Birds Eye Wall's, it hit the share held by Mars Opal Fruits brand and – surprisingly – Mars ice cream. Most important of all, however, Solero achieved its target of expanding the market for ice cream. One quarter of Solero buyers were not previously ice cream impulse buyers at all. For Melanie Heap, Solero's brand manager, the product launch is now history. Her task now is to keep the upward momentum going.

How is the market divided up?

The pattern of replies drawn from market research provides clues as to the kinds of people who are likely to buy that product or service. Several distinct groups of customers are revealed who make up sections or **segments** within the total market. Once the characteristics and buying behaviour of these groups is known, marketing can then be directed at the particular segments or **target groups** which have been identified as containing the most potential customers.

The firm can then establish its market position by concentrating the marketing effort on the particular segment which is likely to yield the highest sales for its products or services. The advantage of identifying target groups is that the sales effort can be directed by means of a 'rifle shot' approach at the people who are most likely to buy. This is far more effective than aiming the sales effort at the market in general, as in the scattered 'shotgun' approach.

Market segments are divided up on the basis of demographic factors, such as age, sex and geographical area, and also on consumers' income, occupation and ethnic group. Segments can also be divided up in terms of many other factors, such as whether people are heavy or light users of the product or service.

One of the most common ways of defining market segments is by **socio-economic group (SEG)**. Table 2.2 on page 17 illustrates this. People within the same SEG tend to show certain similarities in their expectations, values and behaviour compared with members of other groups. However, this is a very general classification and some overlapping does occur. For example, some people from the lower SEGs may earn more than those from higher SEGs.

The markets for most **fast-moving consumer goods** tend to be highly segmented, for example, soaps, shampoos, cigarettes, biscuits etc. Some companies try to offer a range of products which exploits all segments. However, they need to be aware of the danger of **fragmentation**. This occurs if they try to cater for too many segments, and each segment becomes so small that very little profit is generated.

Small firms generally find it easier to break into a specific segment of a wider market. This enables them to survive by concentrating on supplying a specialised product or service, rather than trying to compete with bigger firms who have cornered the mass market. This strategy of identifying a specialist segment at which marketing can be targeted is called **niche marketing**.

Markets should, however, always be segmented on the basis of what customers want or need, not on the basis of the products they buy. This is an important distinction. Firms who think they are just in the business of making slide rules and concentrate all their efforts on improving their slide rules are in danger of going out of business when a firm comes along which makes calculators. They have ignored the fact that what customers actually want is a product that carries out calculations quickly. They do not want a slide rule as such, so if a better product becomes available which does calculations quickly, consumers will buy that instead.

TABLE 2.2 *JICNARS social grade definitions*

Social grade	Social status	Occupation
A	Upper middle class	Higher managerial, administrative, or professional
B	Middle class	Intermediate managerial, administrative or professional
C1	Lower middle class	Supervisory or clerical, and junior managerial, administrative or professional
C2	Skilled working class	Skilled manual workers
D	Working class	Semi-skilled and unskilled manual workers
E	Those at lowest level of subsistence	State pensioners or widows (no other earner), casual or lowest-grade workers

Source: *JICNARS National Readership Survey*

ACTIVITY

Identifying target groups

I Decide what target group each of the following products or services is aimed at and the needs which are being catered for in each case.

- Spray furniture polish
- Building society accounts
- Ford Fiestas
- Ready meals
- Rolls Royces
- TV rental shops
- *Oh Boy!* magazine
- Polyfilla
- Life insurance
- Season tickets
- The *Financial Times*

2 What are some of the market arguments for the following products or services?

- Shampoos (e.g., normal, dry, greasy, permed, dandruff, frequent wash, baby shampoo etc.)
- Breakfast cereals
- Package holidays
- CDs
- Cheap Day returns
- Cars
- Watches

Who are a firm's main customers?

In many cases, it is common to find that 20 per cent of customers account for 80 per cent of sales. This is known as the 80/20 Rule or **Pareto Effect**.

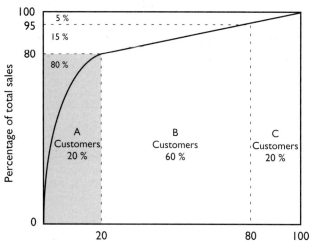

The Pareto Effect

The diagram shows the typical ratio of sales to customer groups found in the Pareto Effect. The A group constitutes 20 per cent of customers and accounts for 80 per cent of total sales. The B group constitutes 60 per cent of customers and accounts for 15 per cent of sales, whilst the C group makes up 20 per cent of customers, but only accounts for 5 per cent of sales. Clearly, firms that are successful in identifying the A group can make their advertising considerably more effective by targeting these important customers. However, they should not forget that some B or C group customers can become A group customers with good service and attention.

The marketing mix

After considering the market research findings and identifying the market segment it intends to target, the firm then needs to offer a total package to meet customers' needs and wants. Four key areas are blended to produce the required response in the target audience: product, price, place and promotion. These elements make up the **marketing mix**, or 'offering' to the customer.

The right product

A new product is distinct from a **line extension**, such as a 'new' lemon version of a shampoo. Ideas for new products can come from anywhere – the company's own research and development programme, competitors' products and so on. A constant supply of new ideas or **concepts** is needed, as only a small percentage survives screening and test marketing to be launched nationally.

Sometimes it takes marketing flair to think of a good use for an invention. The highly successful yellow Post-it™ notes were born when 3M invented an adhesive that had low stickiness but retained its properties after repeated use. It wasn't what they were looking for so it was put on the shelf, until years later when another researcher suggested using it for a notepad with pages that stuck but could be peeled off easily. Post-it™ notes went on to become one of their best sellers – quite a feat in view of the fact that 3M make about 60,000 different products!

Of course, only a handful of new products ever become winners. One reason many products fail is that they are not distinctive enough. If a new product is to succeed, it should have certain features which make it stand out from the competition, so that it forms a **unique selling proposition (USP)**. In reality, these distinguishing features are often very minor. For instance, all shampoos contain the same basic ingredients. It is only the additives which vary slightly. The differences are more in the way each shampoo is packaged, priced and advertised. Creating a unique identity in this way turns a product into a **brand**, which means it can then be sold for more. A comparison between prices of branded goods and supermarket own-label goods illustrates the point.

Companies can increase their total **market share** by introducing many **brand variants** aimed at different segments of the market. For example, Van den Berghs have done this with their margarine brands, such as Stork, Blue Band, Echo, Flora, Krona etc. However, firms must be careful not to introduce brands with a low profit margin that **cannibalise** market share away from their other products which may be brand leaders with higher profit margins.

THE PRODUCT LIFE CYCLE

Any product will pass through various stages in its life cycle, just as humans and animals do, although the time span between when it is first introduced and when it is finally withdrawn from the market varies greatly.

As products reach maturity in a market which has been fully exploited and has therefore become **saturated**, they start to decline. In some cases, the firm may decide to delay the end by using various **extension strategies**. The product can be given a new lease of life by being repackaged or reformulated. A good example of a long-running brand is Lux soap which is over 80 years old. Its

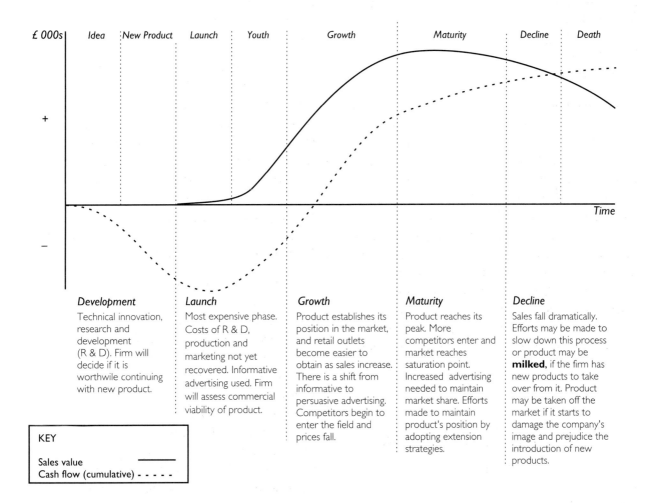

£ 000s | Idea | New Product | Launch | Youth | Growth | Maturity | Decline | Death

Development
Technical innovation, research and development (R & D). Firm will decide if it is worthwile continuing with new product.

Launch
Most expensive phase. Costs of R & D, production and marketing not yet recovered. Informative advertising used. Firm will assess commercial viability of product.

Growth
Product establishes its position in the market, and retail outlets become easier to obtain as sales increase. There is a shift from informative to persuasive advertising. Competitors begin to enter the field and prices fall.

Maturity
Product reaches its peak. More competitors enter and market reaches saturation point. Increased advertising needed to maintain market share. Efforts made to maintain product's position by adopting extension strategies.

Decline
Sales fall dramatically. Efforts may be made to slow down this process or product may be **milked**, if the firm has new products to take over from it. Product may be taken off the market if it starts to damage the company's image and prejudice the introduction of new products.

KEY

Sales value ———
Cash flow (cumulative) - - - - -

The product life cycle

shape, perfume, colour and packaging have changed continuously during that time. Other strategies include finding new uses or markets for the product or bringing out new accessories for it.

Some brands seem to live forever – your parents and maybe even your grandparents will probably remember such classics as Bisto, Oxo, Dettol, Ovaltine, or Colman's mustard.

Most products do, of course, eventually die. Often this is just because of changing consumer tastes, but increasingly it is because of the rapid pace of technological change. Life cycles are getting shorter and shorter, especially in areas such as the electronics industry. New products become obsolete; often within months rather than years, as each technically more advanced version is brought out.

THE BOSTON MATRIX

A single-product business is very vulnerable in the market place, particularly if it only has a few major customers. Most businesses are therefore **multi-product** firms with a **portfolio** or variety of products, which they try to ensure are all at different stages in their life cycles in order to avoid great fluctuations in profit levels. A well-balanced portfolio also means that the revenue generated by older products can help to nurture new products through their introduction.

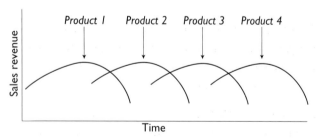

Note: In reality most firms will have groups of products rather than individual products.

The importance of successive product launches

The Boston Consulting Group in Massachusetts, USA, have devised a matrix for classifying products in order to analyse whether a firm's product portfolio is well balanced.

The Boston Matrix

The right price

The price of a product or service is another element of the marketing mix, which interacts with the other factors to determine whether or not consumers will buy. The model of demand and supply in the diagram shows how the market works.

This overall view of the market provides a simple view of how demand and supply interact. However, a firm's decision as to which pricing strategy to adopt is complicated by many other factors. The pricing strategy will vary according to the stage reached in the product's life cycle and its **position** in the market relative to its competitors. If the product can be **differentiated** from rival products, perhaps by its good design, or by the quality of the after-sales service offered, then it can be sold for more.

So what pricing strategies might be used?

● **Market penetration** A price is set which is below that of competitors, in order to capture a share of the market. A short-term loss is sometimes accepted, in the hope that the price can be raised after **brand loyalty** has been gained and customers start to reorder the brand by name. The actual products may be priced cheaply in order to encourage customers to buy,

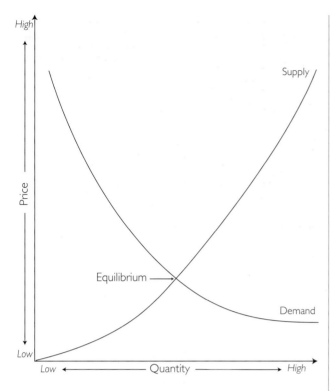

Demand curve – shows more goods are bought when prices are low.
Supply curve – shows suppliers offer more goods when prices are high.
Equilibrium – the market price is set where supply equals demand.
Glut – when an excess of supply pushes prices down.
Shortage – when supply is too low to meet the demand, forcing prices up.

Supply and demand curves

but the accessories to go with it may be priced expensively, as with the film for instant cameras. However, if prices are pitched too low, customers may become suspicious about quality. Another danger of price cutting is that competitors may retaliate by lowering their prices as well. Firms tend to avoid getting into such a price-cutting war, because the end result is that they all achieve the same market share as they had before, but at a lower price level. A low price strategy may also prove dangerous for products which are expected to have a short life span.

● **Skimming**   A high price is set to recover the development costs of new products quickly. Consumers are prepared to pay high prices for products which are innovative and for which there are no substitutes. CD players, for example, were priced at £1,000 when first launched, yet within two years were available for £200. Similarly, video recorders, calculators, computer

games and telephone answering machines all commanded high prices when they were first introduced onto the market. The danger of pricing products too highly is that sales may be lost.

● **Price discrimination**   A price is set which varies for different segments of the market – for example, pensioners can get cheap tickets.

● **Competitive pricing**   A price is set which is at the same going rate as competitors' prices. This is common when goods or services provided are very similar and not capable of being differentiated very much, as with home mortgages or petrol.

Having worked out their pricing strategy, firms then need to calculate what price to charge for their goods. A common pricing method is **cost plus**, which is when the total costs incurred are added together and a suitable percentage **mark-up** added on for profit. In the final analysis, though, the 'right' price should not just be based on the firm's costs. It must relate to the price that sufficient numbers of customers are prepared to pay – that is, the price that the market will bear – which in turn is dependent on how customers perceive the value of the product.

The right place

Having decided on the right product and price, the company has to get the product to the industrial user or final consumer by way of an efficient and cost-effective distribution system.

The traditional **channel of distribution** is from manufacturer to wholesaler to retailer to consumer. Wholesalers, because they are in the middle, have the advantage of **breaking bulk**. This means that retailers can buy in smaller quantities from them, rather than from manufacturers who tend to prefer to make one large delivery.

In recent years this chain has been shortened as many manufacturers have started to sell directly to large retailers who buy in bulk, such as the supermarket chains with their own depots, or to retailers who can carry huge stocks themselves, such as the hypermarkets like Asda. A shorter distribution channel is also used when the product is fragile and handling must be minimised, as with frozen foods, or where the product is bulky, as with furniture. Some manufacturers sell directly to the consumer using mail order.

The method of transport is also important. Cost-effective physical distribution can result in significant savings for the company. The choice of transport method is determined by weight, bulk, value and perishability of the goods and by the needs of the company. Road tends to be the most popular as it is the most flexible method, offering a door-to-door service without the restrictions of rail transport. Rail is cheaper for bulky goods and can compete with road over long journeys where the door-to-door factor becomes less critical. Air is used for light, expensive and perishable goods. Sea is used for bulky commodities like oil transported over long distances. In recent years the widespread use of containers has streamlined distribution considerably.

The choice of **distribution outlet** is partly influenced by the image and nature of the product. Expensive perfume would obviously not be sold through supermarkets. Products that have a low unit cost, are purchased frequently and are easily substituted, such as crisps and baked beans, must be widely available or sales are lost.

Retail outlets include supermarkets, hypermarkets, department stores, multiple stores, cooperatives and discount stores. Goods can also be sold by mail order and door-to-door selling. A recent development has been the growth of **franchising**, where the **franchisees** own their own business but the **franchiser** provides the name, products and expertise to run it, with the benefits of economies of scale like bulk buying and national advertising.

The Body Shop group provides a good example of the benefits of franchising where the franchiser is able to expand by functioning, in effect, as a wholesaler. Anita Roddick, 1984's Businesswoman of the Year, has made her Body Shop group something of a retailing legend, with sales accelerating to £195 million in 1994 and numerous applicants waiting for a franchise. With only £4,000 start-up capital, she has managed to expand the business through the franchise route, yet still kept tight control on all the outlets.

The right promotion

Having got the right product and determined the right price the firm must design an effective promotion strategy. There are three aspects of promotion: advertising, sales promotions and public relations.

ADVERTISING

This is the most common type of promotion and one of the earliest forms. As mass production increased in the latter stages of the Industrial Revolution and economies of scale were made, high volume sales were needed, which meant firms had to advertise in order to attract large numbers of customers. As living standards improved still further, encouraging the production of more goods, it was no longer a sellers' market and firms had to compete with each other to persuade customers to buy their product.

Not all advertising is aimed at consumers as the **end users**. Increasingly, advertisers are having to sell to the retailer, which necessitates a different kind of advertising, where the degree of trade acceptability already achieved by the product is emphasised in order to persuade the retailer to stock it.

In the field of industrial marketing, the text of advertisements or **advertising copy** tends to be less emotive and more informative. This is because industrial buying decisions often tend to be made by groups of people rather than individuals, unlike those made by domestic consumers. The decisions also tend to be made in a more formal and methodical way. There is a greater emphasis on advertising in the trade press, trade fairs and exhibitions and on the use of technical brochures.

Commercial television is the most expensive medium to use but is also the most popular because of its effectiveness. Although TV advertising in Britain is only 40 years old, it has produced slogans and catch phrases that have become part of our language, familiar jingles and lasting images. The demands of telling an interesting story in a short space of time are such that it is no accident that one of our most successful directors, Alan Parker of *Bugsy Malone*, *Midnight Express* and *Shoot the Moon* fame, began in films as a director of TV commercials.

Other media that are less expensive include commercial radio, posters, cinema, magazines, journals and newspapers.

ACTIVITY

Identifying types of advertising

Give examples of products and services which are advertised by using the following methods:

- **Persuasive** – glamorous images and persuasive language used to encourage consumers to buy.

- **Informative** – used to make consumers aware of the existence and identity of the product. May provide technical information.

- **Corporate** – where a company promotes its name and image rather than an individual product. Benefits overall sales of all products.

- **Generic** – where a group of manufacturers promotes a whole industry or type of product.

- **Competitive** – where companies subtly imply that rival firms' products are inferior to their own.

SALES PROMOTIONS

These are used to generate short-term increases in sales by encouraging consumers to try the product once, in the hope of generating repeat sales. They include:

- Coupons, vouchers, and percentage reduction (such as 25p off, £1 cash refund, etc.).
- Free samples. These are often used for new products.
- Self-liquidating offers. Goods are offered at cost price for a certain number of tokens or packet tops.
- Free offers, such as free gifts at petrol stations.
- Bargain packs such as '20 per cent extra free', 'Buy two, get one free' etc.
- Charity promotions. On receipt of a certain number of proofs of purchase, a donation is made to charity.
- Prize promotions and newspaper bingo.

Point-of-sale promotions encourage customers into the shop. A well-known type of price promotion is the use of **loss leaders**, where customers are attracted into the shop by a few products priced cheaply in the hope that they will then buy other products priced normally.

PUBLIC RELATIONS

This is the process of obtaining favourable publicity via the editorial columns of press media or in television or radio braodcasts. The PR expert has the contacts within the media to ensure that the client's story or side to a dispute is reported sympathetically. Public relations can be a positive process of organising interviews on Breakfast TV shows or setting up launch parties for new products. However there have also been cases where PR personnel have been engaged in spreading negative, even malicious stories about rival firms. PR can also backfire if it is *too* successful. For example, some pop bands are so 'hyped' that their music cannot live up to the advance publicity.

CASE STUDY

Levi 501s – why was denim fading?

The scene is an American laundromat in the 1950s. A young man wearing jeans walks in, calmly takes off his jeans and puts them in the machine. He then sits down amongst the other customers in his boxer shorts and carries on reading while he waits for his jeans to be washed.

This advert, 'Launderette', which was part of the campaign that advertising agency Bartle Bogle Hegarty (BBH) produced for the relaunched Levi 501s, has become a cult classic – one of the most successful adverts of all time. It made the actor, Nick Kamen, an overnight star. In the UK alone, sales rocketed by 800 per cent within the first year. The factory in Scotland where the jeans were stitched together could not meet demand, even by working 18-hour shifts and taking on extra staff. Levi's sold three months' stock of 501s in just three weeks. Shops were besieged by people asking to try on the jeans that 'the bloke in the launderette wears'.

Yet before the decision was taken to relaunch the original 501 classic design, Levi Strauss, who are the world's biggest manufacturer of jeans, were suffering from a serious downturn in the jeans market. The main problem was that by the early 1980s, the 16- to 24-year-olds who buy half of all jeans sold had begun to see denim jeans as a tired legacy of their parents' younger years. Sales in the European jeans market slumped from 250 million pairs in 1981 to 150 million pairs in 1985. Levi's reaction to the declining market was to **diversify** their product base. The trouble was that having moved away from jeans into products ranging from socks to flannel shirts, it got to the point where the Levi's brand name was in danger of being diluted.

Something had to be done. Levi's made the bold decision to go back to basics, reverse the

diversification and concentrate on selling jeans. The job of designing the European promotion to accompany the relaunch of the 501 design was given to BBH. The objectives of the campaign were to increase the profitability of the company and to lower the age profile of the brand's consumers, which had been creeping up and away from the **core** of the jeans market as the brand's image had worsened. According to Tim Lindsay, the director in charge of the Levi Strauss account at BBH, 'The **creative brief** was to persuade the 15- to 20-year-old males, who represent the core of the jeans market, that 501s were the right look and the only label.' The campaign had to be designed to appeal to this **target market**. The message also had to be clear without the use of speech, as the adverts were to be shown across Europe.

Market research carried out by BBH revealed a growing desire amongst the young for clothes and objects with a genuine heritage. They also uncovered a fascination for a mythical America of the past – 'the America that had produced Dean and Presley, the '57 Chevrolet and Sam Cooke'.

Further research confirmed that the campaign based around the fifties nostalgia theme was liked. Accordingly 'Launderette' and 'Bath' (with actor James Mardle getting into a bath to shrink his 501s) went on air in December 1985. They were quickly followed by 'Parting' and 'Entrance'. The later commercials, 'Cochrane', 'Refrigerator' and 'Pick up', also invoke the nostalgia theme.

The series of commercials for 501s has won many industry awards, both in the UK and internationally. They have been discussed on 23 different TV programmes, thus providing additional free advertising. Most importantly, the campaign achieved its original objectives of returning the company to profitability and of adjusting the brand's **consumer profile** back to the core of the market.

In addition, Levi's **market share** rocketed from 13 per cent to 18 per cent. Competitors did not complain. They also benefited from the rejuvenated jeans market, which expanded from being worth £550 million in 1985 to £800 million in 1987. Sales of other products also increased. The 'golden oldies' which

A scene from Levi's advertisement, 'Creek'

formed the soundtracks of the adverts all got into the UK top ten when re-released. According to trade sources, 'Launderette' also created a major fashion trend, with over two million pairs of boxer shorts being sold in 1986!

Since then, Levi's have cemented their position as market leaders, gaining a 26 per cent share of a market worth £1.11 billion by 1994. The campaign has also gone from strength to strength, with the series of advertisements 'Night and Day', 'Procession', 'Tackle' and 'Campfire' capturing the mood and style of modern day America.

'Creek', focusing on a staid Middle American Sunday picnic opens with a Ma, Pa and their two daughters in a horse-drawn buggy. Enjoying a few moments of

freedom, as they run through the woods the girls are stopped in their tracks by the sight of a bare-torsoed man bathing in the creek and a pair of trousers drying on a rock in the sun. From their hiding place the girls watch as our hero wades to the shore and it is revealed that he is wearing a pair of original shrink-to-fit Levi's 501s.

Industrial marketing

Industrial marketing means offering the right product at the right price at the right place to sell profitably to *business* customers. In other words, selling goods and services that are not aimed directly at consumers.

Industrial marketing is used for:

- Selling finished goods such as aeroplanes, lorries or office furniture.
- Selling raw materials or components such as steel or plastic computer casings.
- Selling services to businesses, such as waste disposal or legal and auditing services.

In any of the above, industrial marketing is likely to imply a finely targeted approach – honing in on the few people in companies who will be involved in making the buying decision. So whereas consumer marketing tends to aim at mass markets, industrial marketing is more focused. A single industrial customer may be responsible for buying millions of pounds worth of a single product.

So how does industrial marketing differ from consumer marketing? Clearly the marketing mix will be affected. When dealing with fewer, more expert buyers, products must be tailored precisely to customer requirements and provide exceptional levels of quality, service back-up and reliability. With industrial marketing, the product becomes the primary element of the mix; although price and place remain very important, promotion often takes a secondary role.

Increasingly, though, progressive British companies are rethinking their approach to the promotion of industrial goods. They have come to appreciate that to keep existing customers and develop new ones requires more innovation and product development. New products can only generate new business if customers are made aware of the developments and their benefits. That can eventually be achieved through salesforce links with existing clients, but product promotion through direct mail, trade exhibitions and trade magazines can also be highly effective.

Many of Britain's biggest and most successful manufacturing companies sell exclusively to industrial buyers. Therefore the general public are unaware of names such as the TI Group, GKN or GEC Alsthom. Yet they are among Britain's biggest export earners and heaviest investors in research and development. Industrial marketing is their way of sustaining this success.

CASE STUDY

Railtrack – changing track

Railtrack is a relatively new company which was formed following the privatization of British Rail. The company is responsible for the track, the signals and signal boxes and the land required by the train operators. Revenue is earned through companies like Virgin who operate the West-Coast passenger line. Virgin pays a 'track access charge' for the use of the track, signals and the required facilities necessary to operate a train service. Being a privatized utility and operating as a monopoly carries certain responsibilities.

One of the responsibilities of Railtrack is that the company is answerable to its shareholders and to the Regulator, as prescribed by the Government when Railtrack was established. This means that there is another factor influencing how it conducts its business. A company with shareholders will normally act to maximize profits to ensure the shareholders are satisfied. However, there are instances when

Railtrack may have to act against this particular stakeholder if, as a consequence of their actions, it fails to meet the Regulator's prescribed guidelines. The diagram on page 27 illustrates the various stakeholders that affect Railtrack.

Apart from the revenue earned from the passenger market, the other main area of track access business is freight, which consists of moving goods from A to B. A significant part of the market is occupied by three main customers who operate a freight service. The largest of these is English Welsh & Scottish Railway (EWS), with 90 per cent of the present market share. Promoting the market for freight transport is one of Railtrack's major objectives, though as yet the market is relatively small; in 1997 only 6 per cent of all freight was transported by rail.

The English, Welsh and Scottish Company transporting coal by rail

One of Railtrack's potential sources of business is to act on behalf of customers wishing to move goods; if a large or regular distributor of goods contacts Railtrack, the latter can either put the distributor in touch with one of the freight operators who will provide everything for the customer, including the wagons to carry the goods, the locomotive, driver and the appropriate access to the route required, or Railtrack can offer a 'track access agreement' directly to the customer, leaving the customer to use a freight operator to provide the locomotive and wagons (see diagram p. 27).

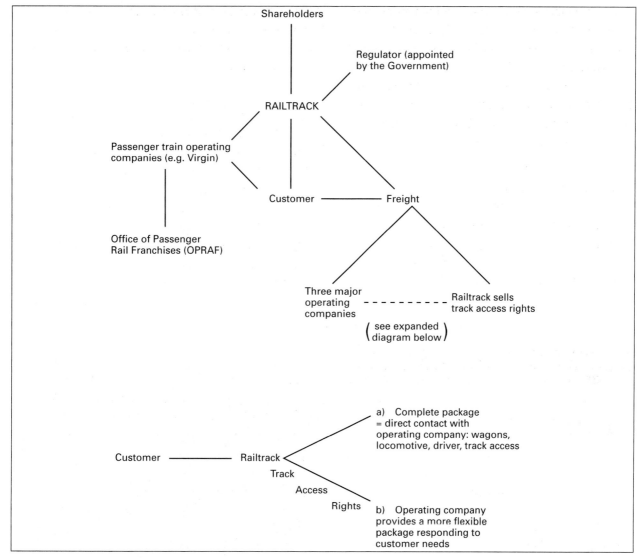

Stakeholders in Railtrack

A further constraint is that although there are plenty of opportunities to expand the freight market, it must be done without disruption to the existing passenger flows.

Upon privatization, the Regulator highlighted the need to change the image of the freight business. Railtrack recognized that the freight industry's perception of themselves was of a non-caring, unreliable, expensive, unresponsive company, unable to communicate effectively. Therefore, the marketing task, apart from increasing revenue, was to transform this image into a user-friendly business which listened to its customers and generated customer confidence by ensuring it provided punctual services at the right price.

Market research confirmed this initial perception; in response, Railtrack produced a *10-point plan* in an attempt to rectify the situation.

1 Reduction in costs (to be more competitive with road transport)
Railtrack has stated that it is committed to a cost reduction plan and where this has been achieved, it has been done so without compromising safety (another factor for operational consideration).

2 Better routes for freight
In an attempt to provide a realistic alternative to the ever more congested road routes.

3 Service improvements – delay reductions
With greater congestion on the motorways, a

reliable rail service would be a distinct advantage.

4 **Service improvements – reduction in transit times**

Another potential advantage over road transport.

5 **Development of freight terminals**

Investing in existing and new sites to meet the needs of its customers' requirements.

6 **Development of the Piggyback project**

A project to enable larger (wider and higher) freight to be transported from the Channel Tunnel to London, the Midlands and the North.

7 **Improved project management**

With so many new projects taking place within the rail network, there is the need for a well-organized management structure that can effectively coordinate and communicate with all the interested bodies that are affected.

8 **Development of open access**

By making it easier for new companies to enter the rail freight business and as a consequence improve the level of competition.

9 **Systems development**

By improving their information systems, it will enable them to offer a better service to the customer.

10 **Code of Practice**

This sets out a number of key commitments of Railtrack in order to promote the rail freight industry. Railtrack wanted the Code to be an indication to the transport industry as to the way it operates (to be viewed as a mission statement).

In addition, they produced:

The Railtrack Freight Connections Guide

This is a summary of all existing facilities (1700 locations throughout the country). Such information, e.g. terminals, sidings, capacity and yards, coupled with their ownership details, is seen as vital in developing the rail freight industry.

A Route Directory

This is made available in a booklet allowing the operating companies to plan their route, taking into consideration the physical constraints along any given route (gauge access). It provides details of the width and height of tunnels and bridges, (not track width). Potential customers, with a variety of different sized freight wagons, were unaware of which could be used on which route. Consequently Railtrack published:

Which route for which gauge

This acted as a sales brochure. It was quickly followed by the CD Rom version, issued in December 1997.

RAILTRACK SUCCESSES TO DATE

Success to date has meant a greater utilization of existing capacity, carrying a wider range of goods. Railtrack is, however, waiting for the big breakthrough. It is too early to tell if the 10-point plan will be a success; they have laid out their objectives and made great efforts to inform the consumer of the services available. The 4 'P's of marketing have been clearly considered and ought to bring success in the very near future.

Railtrack is adamant that it has arrested the decline in rail traffic, brought about by the emergence of larger lorries, the lack of modernization by what was British Rail, that led to ever increasing costs and an inability to take note of what the customer required.

The following is an example of one of the success stories to date.

Eddie Stobart, the Carlisle-based road haulier is hoping to be operating a rail freight service by the middle of 1998. The company is planning to operate a service between Daventry and Glasgow and has indicated that several companies have expressed an interest in the proposed service.

The haulier has started procedures for the purchase of the appropriate rail wagons, similar to those that operate between Swindon and Longbridge carrying components for Rover.

In addition, Eddie Stobart is contemplating the acquisition of a warehouse facility at the Europark at Gwent in South Wales, where a new rail terminal is being planned.

ACTIVITY

Pace Designs: designing a promotional campaign for a new product

BRIEF

You work for the advertising agency of Marston, Davis and Longton, who have just been approached by Pace Designs to produce a new promotion campaign for the national launch of their exciting new range of unisex jeans aimed at the 16- to 24-year-old target group.

1   Decide on a new name for the jeans and an appropriate slogan to be used in all the promotions. These must be in keeping with the image of the product and its market positioning.

2   Two commercials will be produced by your agency, to be shown on TV and in the cinema, which will cost £300,000 each to make. Suggest an outline idea or theme on which the adverts could be based.

3   Decide how you will allocate your promotion budget of £1.5 million between TV and press in order to reach the target group most effectively. Use the tables on page 31, which show advertising rates and circulation figures. Decide if any other sales promotions are to be used.

4   Design a full-page advertising spread for a newspaper or magazine, based on the theme you have chosen and incorporating all the necessary details.

 ## DISCUSSION POINTS

1 *Every business has many stakeholders (groups with an interest in the firm's success or failure). Which of the following stakeholders are affected by Railtrack's marketing success?*
- *Shareholders*
- *Employees*
- *The Government*
- *Road transport companies*
- *Companies requiring goods to be transported*

2 *Many people think that the interests of stakeholders inevitably conflict. Discuss this view in the light of the Railtrack case study.*

Advertising rates for selected TV regions

ITV Region	Maximum cost of a 30 second spot at weekday peak times (£)	Audience (number of ITV households '000)
Carlton/LWT (London)	74,000	4,565
Central TV (Midlands)	35,000	3,668
Granada TV (North West)	21,000	2,590
Yorkshire TV (Yorkshire)	15,000	2,301
Meridian (South and South East)	28,000	2,134
HTV (Wales and West)	15,000	1,842
Anglia TV (East)	20,000	1,665
Scottish TV (Central Scotland)	11,000	1,400
Tyne Tees TV (North East)	5,000	1,184
West Country TV (South West)	6,000	660
Ulster TV (Ulster)	3,000	491
Grampian TV (North Scotland)	2,000	479
Border TV (Border)	1,200	271

Source: British Rate and Data (BRAD), June 1994, BARB Establishment Survey Report Q4 1993

Advertising rates for selected TV regions

Newspaper or magazine	Cost of full page (£) *1	Circulation (average sales per month)*2
Daily Express	20,825	1,220,055
Daily Mail	26,208	2,151,207
Daily Mirror	27,500	2,390,208
Sun	34,700	3,842,376
Daily Telegraph	38,500	1,133,931
News of the World	38,300	4,365,032
Radio Times	13,700	1,405,862
TV Times	9,600	981,811
Cosmopolitan (colour)	13,560	461,080
Mizz (colour)	5,210	138,381
Just Seventeen	7,930	130,080
Options	5,150	146,692

Source: British Rate and Data (BRAD)
*1 July 1997,
*2 April 1997

Advertising rates for selected newspapers and magazines

Design and development

IN ASSOCIATION WITH

SONY

Introduction: what does design involve?

In the face of mounting evidence that buying decisions are rarely made on price alone, it is becoming increasingly obvious that good design is a powerful and competitive weapon for business. Good design can also add value to a product, enabling it to be sold for more. Enlightened firms are already realising that good design can be one of the most powerful forces in creating distinctiveness, not just in terms of the features or look of the product, but also in terms of its quality and performance.

Good industrial design can influence not just what a product looks like, but how easily and cheaply it is made, how efficiently and reliably it functions and how well it can be displayed at the point of sale. Product design is therefore not only about **form** and **aesthetics** – that is, shape and appearance – but also about **function** – that is, performance. However, industrial designers can only contribute fully if they are given a pivotal role in the development team rather than just being brought in as stylists at the end. They should be fully involved in every stage of the development process right through to advising on tooling and production systems.

Ideally, designers should work towards meeting a **design brief** or specification that describes the criteria or standards which the product design should achieve; though inevitably, any product design always represents a compromise solution between all the factors which have had to be reconciled. It is also influenced by a variety of constraints which place limitations on the designer.

Paul Kotler, in a recent article, 'Design: A powerful strategic tool', argues that in order to succeed a company must 'seek to creatively blend the major elements of the **design mix**, namely performance, quality, durability, appearance and cost'.

Concorde – this design has taken into account function as well as form and aesthetics (© Adrian Meredith)

ACTIVITY

Analysing the factors involved in designing a new product

Look at the questions below, which might be asked by a design team working on a new product. State which element of the design mix is being considered in each one.

● How will inspection and testing for faults be carried out?

● Is the styling in keeping with the image of the product?

● Does the product have the latest technical functions the market wants?

● Can the design be simplified to make production easier?

● Are the properties of the materials and components suitable for the product's expected life?

● Can fewer moving parts be used?

● Is the product comfortable/practical to use?

● Can this design be made with the existing production facilities?

● Will the investment in the product be recovered over its life cycle?

● How good are the materials and components from suppliers?

● What are the distinguishing features of the product's exterior?

● How regularly will the product need maintenance/servicing?

● What operating/storage conditions will the product have to stand up to?

● Are the materials and components in line with the retail price?

● What safety standards and regulations will the product have to comply with?

● Can maintenance be carried out easily?

CASE STUDY

Design-based innovation at Sony

Explorers may have proved that the world is round but Sony believe that perfection is completely flat as in their new completely flat screen television, the FD Trinitron WEGA.

Since the very first Sony TV was made available in 1960, the company has been at the forefront of audio / visual technology and has been committed to developing new and more innovative products. The introduction of the Sony Trinitron colour CRT (cathode ray tube) in 1968 is a very good example which won the prestigious Emmy Award for Outstanding Technological Development in 1973. Sony Trinitron technology is now the benchmark for computer graphic display monitors. With a vertically flat screen, it offered a level of picture clarity and sharpness necessary for today's fast moving communications world, but more importantly, the development of the Sony Trinitron was the first step towards the ultimate goal of a completely flat screen TV.

BUT WHY IS THE FLAT SCREEN SO SUPERIOR?

It was widely accepted that the flat screen would give a far superior picture quality with zero image distortion, less reflection and a far wider viewing angle, but it was always thought to be technically impossible, and for two very good reasons:

1 Physics

For an image to appear on the television screen, cathode rays are shot from a cathode gun, through an electronic aiming device and on to the inside surface of the phosphor-coated screen. The challenge is to get the rays that are travelling to the centre of the screen to react, the same as those travelling the much greater distances to the edges. A curved screen reduces the distance to the edges and makes it easier to achieve a clear, sharp picture across the entire screen.

2 Strength

A CRT is basically a bubble of glass containing a vacuum. An extremely strong design is required to stop the whole thing from collapsing in on itself. As nature has shown (for example an egg) a curved surface is inherently stronger than a flat one.

However, on the one hundredth birthday of the Cathode Ray Tube, Sony made the impossible possible. The world's first completely flat widescreen TV was developed – the **SONY FD TRINITRON**.

HOW DID SONY ACHIEVE THIS REMARKABLE FEAT?

The project for developing the flat screen TV was launched in 1995 with the mission: 'To develop a completely flat CRT (cathode ray tube) to introduce the product in time for Christmas Sales in 1996.' By any standards this would be a tight schedule, but for such an innovative design as the completely-flat screen television this time-scale was thought to be almost impossible. The project was named 'Mission Impossible Nomura' after the project leader, Mr K. Nomura.

Due to the impossibly tight time allowed for this project it became a Top Policy and was given top priority over everything else, what is known at Sony as a Top Down Directive. It had to be completed in time for the 50th anniversary of Sony in 1996. So how is a Top Down Directive developed? A project leader and team members were selected, all well experienced and trained by Sony and the project leader was given full authority to proceed without having to defer decisions to other management areas.

Development of this project was approached before the actual project announcement was made. The project leader made a daily schedule for 150 days ahead so that the workforce could be completely motivated and would have specific targets. These targets were:

● To produce the first completely flat CRT in the business.
● To achieve the shortest time for completion to on-line.
● To use 'Positive Spiral Thinking', i.e. never giving up and concentrating on achieving the end result.

The design of this revolutionary new television was started before the actual technical development of

Impossible sound

Impossibly flat

Impossible design

the CRT was completed. It was therefore vitally important to have good communications between the CRT side and the TV side. The development for the key technology of the flat panel was confirmed while the actual design was proceeding. This technical development was focused on achieving the customer's requirements in the shortest time. Throughout the development period, the schedule was kept under tight control which meant keeping one step ahead all the time and planning the next step of the project whilst working on the current stage. Whilst evaluating the CRT the team thought about when and which parts should be ordered for the next prototype.

Amazingly, and against all odds Sony made the impossible possible and the prototype was completed in time for the Sony anniversary in 1996. The project was named 'WEGA' after the double star in the constellation of Lyra. It is one of the brightest stars that exists and became a benchmark to measure the brightness of all stars. In the same way, Sony are sure that WEGA TV will be used as a benchmark for other TVs.

A completely flat screen has always been thought to be an impossibility but that did not stop Sony from creating one. Sony has produced a perfect window on the world which provides a picture of absolute clarity and proving that completely flat is perfectly possible.

ACTIVITY

Analysing the stages involved in introducing a new product

Decide on the most logical order for the sequence of events involved in introducing a new product from the list below. What factors could influence the best order?

- Full-scale production
- Working samples made up and tested
- Models or prototypes made up
- Design chosen from concepts presented
- Design brief for product prepared
- Patent applied for
- Consumer trials on target group carried out
- Original idea or concept
- Gap in market identified
- Own designers or outside consultants from design agency approached
- Raw materials organised
- Tooling made up for manufacture
- Market research on consumer needs carried out

Products must satisfy consumer needs

The first requirement of a successful new product is that it must be geared to satisfying consumer needs. However, this is more easily said than done. In affluent western societies today, a vast range of products and services exists to serve consumer needs. Many innovative firms are therefore going one stage further by attempting to stimulate subconscious needs. This new focus is evident in the approach adopted by one company, (quoted by the DTI in their survey of innovative companies), who argue that, 'You must get into the mind of the customer even when the customer does not know their own mind!' The challenge now facing marketers is that these **latent needs** are awakened only when the new product is first introduced onto the market. After all, how many people thought they needed a personal stereo, compact disc player or microwave oven until these products actually became available?

In his book, *The Design Dimension*, Christopher Lorenz describes the approach adopted by Sony. When Sony unveiled their new portable black-and-white TV set with an eight-inch screen in the USA during the 1960s, it was an immediate success. Yet only weeks earlier, General Electric had completed a major piece of market research on the potential of small, portable TVs and their findings included conclusions like 'people do not place a high value on portability of the TV set'. Rather than asking consumers to predict their feelings towards an unfamiliar product, Sony had instead observed the growing number of sets sold and the increasing number of TV channels and realised that these two factors would create a demand for a second set in many homes. Lorenz went on to add that, 'In effect, the company had looked beyond consumers expressed needs to their underlying behaviour patterns and had led the market by stimulating a new want. It has since done precisely the same with the video cassette recorder, Walkman™ personal stereo and the Watchman™ flat-tube TV.'

Clearly, companies with a successful record of product innovation are those who consistently manage to introduce products which satisfy the existing or latent needs of a target market. This sounds a very straightforward recipe for success. The fact is there are many pitfalls for the unwary. For one thing, the findings of market research surveys often provide a poor indication of the true sales potential of highly innovative products. It is notoriously difficult to gauge consumer reaction to radically different products which are unlike anything else on the market, since consumers invariably dislike products they cannot visualise.

The example of the Post-it™ notepads developed by 3M is typical, where the marketing people were ready to scrap the project at an early stage because the product had performed so badly in the initial research studies. In this instance, the use of trial samples proved to be the key factor in gaining consumer acceptance and the familiar yellow note-pads have since become one of 3M's most successful products.

Some would argue that if companies always heeded market research findings they would never launch radically different products at all. Certainly the lesson appears to be that damning research findings in the case of innovative products should be treated with a degree of caution in order to avoid the danger of rejecting potential winners. Decisions made on the strength of market research recommendations should, in any case, always be taken in the light of managers' experience and judgement. In the most

innovative companies, their 'feel' for the market is legendary. For instance, the Sony Walkman™ was launched despite research that warned it would be a complete flop. In the event, Sony went on to reap the marketing coup of the decade.

However, these examples do not indicate that market research evidence should be ignored as a matter of course. In the majority of cases properly conducted research is a reliable predictor of market potential. In fact, the penalty for introducing products which have been developed without reference to consumer needs can be high. The Sinclair C5 is a classic example of a product which, although it was extremely innovative, failed within a very short time of being launched. This was largely because the market need for an electronic vehicle with a limited carrying capacity and performance was never properly established.

A full-scale market research survey was out of the question because of the emphasis on secrecy. Instead, a small sample of 63 families was shown the vehicle and allowed to drive it around a large room. The C5 was launched on the basis of this limited research and of course the personal conviction of Sir Clive Sinclair.

In October 1985 the *Financial Times* reported that the receiver put the debts of Sinclair's C5 concern at £7.75 million. Nevertheless, it is interesting to speculate whether the C5 might have succeeded if it had been promoted as a golf trolley or invalid wheelchair. In other words, could it have survived if it had been designed to meet a specific consumer need?

The Sinclair C5

ACTIVITY

Needs catered for by different innovations

What are the needs and requirements catered for by the following innovations?

- Car phones
- Low-calorie drinks
- Cash machines
- Non-stick pans
- Infra-red alarm detectors
- Video-cassette recorders
- Solid emulsion paints
- Personal computers
- Personal stereos
- Disposable kitchen towels
- Frozen ready meals
- High speed trains
- Satellite dishes
- Photocopiers

The role of technology

The pace of technological change is such that new products are quickly superseded as competitors scramble to bring out even more advanced versions. In the nature of things it is inevitable that successful products are going to attract imitators. However, it is the scale of competition today that is unprecedented. As Richard Brookes points out in his book, *The New Marketing*, 'Five years after the launch of its personal computer, IBM was fighting a new battle – not with the Japanese as everyone originally expected, but with low-wage companies in Taiwan and South Korea. By 1986 IBM's PC had become a commodity product and was being copied by more than two hundred firms.'

Firms need, therefore, to introduce a constant stream of new products. Few can aim to be as prolific as Hewlett Packard, who manage to generate ideas for eight new products a week! Yet all the signs suggest that UK firms, particularly in terms of creative ability, have the potential to exceed this performance. A survey by the Japanese Ministry of International Trade and Industry, quoted in *Winning Ways* by James Pilditch, claims that of the significant innovations since the Second World War, 6 per cent were Japanese, 14 per cent were French, 22 per cent came from the USA and a staggering 55 per cent were from the UK.

State-of-the-art technology has certainly been the key factor determining the success of Renishaw Plc, a British manufacturer whose touch-trigger probe is capable of measuring machined steel to accuracies of millionths of a metre. The probe, which has a 70 per cent share of the world market for such tools, is used on products ranging from car engines to the US space shuttle, where the accurate fit of the heat-shielding tiles is vital to the survival of the shuttle as it passes through the earth's atmosphere.

The role of technology is essential in stimulating a high level of innovation, particularly amongst the motor vehicle, electronic, aerospace, pharmaceutical and consumer goods industries. New technological advances can determine:

- **The kinds of products and services that are offered**, e.g. fax machines, satellite TV, digital audio tapes, cash dispensing machines, antibiotics, etc.
- **The kinds of raw materials that are available**, e.g. man-made fibres, biodegradable plastics, ceramic parts for car engines, aseptic packaging for products like fruit juices which previously required refrigeration, etc.
- **The ways in which products are designed and manufactured**, e.g. techniques like CAD have dramatically reduced the time taken to design and engineer new products and the use of robots has revolutionised production lines in industries like car manufacturing.

Given the crucial role played by technology in innovation it is obviously vital that companies keep an open mind towards emerging technologies. In 1938, an amateur physicist living in New York called Chester Carlson developed a process which he called 'electro-photography'. Carlson approached more than 20 companies to try and get them to develop his product, including RCA, IBM and General Electric, but was turned down by every one. Eventually, a small company called Haloid agreed to develop his process commercially. Haloid, which later became Xerox, is now one of the largest corporations in the USA – a success due in no small measure to the fact that the company was the first to spot the huge potential of photocopiers.

Clearly, then, firms need to be flexible enough to respond to each wave of technological progress as it occurs. Ultimately, those who are unwilling or unable to adapt to the rapidly accelerating pace of change are likely to face an increasingly uncertain future – witness the fate of many of the Swiss watchmakers who were slow in adopting quartz digital technology. However, market conditions are complex and there are many reasons why even products that are technologically superior do not automatically succeed. In the case of the Apple Macintosh computer, what should have been a huge sales advantage (that is, that anyone, not just computer experts, could learn how to operate the computer in as little as 20 minutes) counted for very little in a market where the need for IBM compatibility was the major consideration.

order to cater for the latest customer expectations. It is all too easy to get left behind when yesterday's radical new extras, such as VCRs with Nicam digital stereo, become today's taken-for-granted features. The motor car industry illustrates the scale of this competition. Japan's eight car manufacturers change their models on average every 4.6 years. This compares with an average figure of 8.1 years for the three major US car makers and 12.2 years for European manufacturers.

UK firms clearly face a formidable challenge. By definition, those who do not view innovation as a priority have effectively opted for stagnation and eventual decline. The role of management is critical in nurturing a culture that actively fosters change and innovation. 'Our job', according to one chairman of a highly innovative company, 'is to make our products obsolete before our competitors do.' Innovation is often confused with invention and assumed to be the sole province of the research and development (R & D) department. The popular image of boffins in white coats conjuring up new inventions is clearly outdated. The reality is that innovation does not have to be technology-led. People from a wide variety of departments within an organisation are capable of thinking up ideas for new products or modifications to existing products.

The importance of innovation

In the fiercely competitive trading conditions of the 1990s, innovation has emerged as the main battleground, with success being determined by the ability of companies to bring a constant stream of ever-more sophisticated products to the market ahead of their competitors. The rules of the game have moved on. Innovation was once regarded as essential for growth; today it has become essential for survival.

Rising standards of living and the pace of technological change mean that companies need to constantly update their products and services in

Something old, something new

The innovation process is not just about radical new inventions, although these do sometimes occur. The existence of well-known examples of innovations based on *revolutionary* technological changes, such as the invention of robots, fibre optics, lasers and silicon chips, has unfortunately tended to perpetuate the myth that most innovations stem from this kind of creative breakthrough. In fact, the reality behind most product introductions is far less dramatic.

Innovations tend to develop more as a result of an *evolutionary* process: once a product has been introduced onto the market, the information provided as feedback from users is incorporated into later modifications and improvements, through continuous redesigns. The product thus evolves gradually in stages, via a series of small incremental steps, rather than as a giant technical quantum leap forward. The so-called 'blockbuster discoveries' are, by definition, few and far between. After all, radically different products such as the TV, computer or aeroplane cannot be invented very often!

Most 'new' designs have in fact evolved from this process of continuous redesign or **iteration**, which refines the product into a version that is cheaper, offers more sophisticated features and is better designed in some way. Innovation therefore involves modifying old products as well as developing new ones.

Japanese firms, such as Sony, have consistently adopted a policy of re-innovation. In a recent speech, Sony's founder and honorary chairman, Akio Morita, summed up the company's attitude: 'The technology of one product spawns the more advanced technology for another. We would not have been able to develop the Trinitron TV, or compact disc and digital recording, if we had not known how to design and manufacture the generation of products preceding them.' He went on to add that creativity in **product planning** was also important: 'There was no new technology involved in the Sony Walkman. What we did was see the technology we already had in a totally new configuration.'

In this context, it is obviously essential for firms to develop products which are capable of being redesigned. Gardiner and Rothwell, in their report on innovation for the Design Council, distinguish between **lean** and **robust** designs. Robust designs can be stretched to produce a variety of versions for different requirements which form a **product design family**. The Boeing 707 and Ford Cortina are both examples of designs which gradually evolved into a family of models, each new stage incorporating the latest technological developments. Robust designs like this have a greater degree of flexibility than lean designs which are not capable of being adapted when customers need change.

Should firms just stick, then, to redesigning and developing their tried and tested products? Clearly, this offers less financial risk in the short term, but without a flow of new products a company is likely to stagnate and decline. Companies need, obviously, to get the balance right between revamping old products and introducing new ones. Manufacturers of coated products, 3M, who have a formidable reputation for innovation, demonstrate what can be achieved. With about 60,000 individual products ranging from Scotch™ tape to Post-it™ notes, they consistently achieve their target of deriving 27 per cent of their sales revenue each year from products or services that are less than five years old.

CASE STUDY

Sony – the news studio in a briefcase

When watching a TV news reporter, how do you think the pictures got to you? Remember that they may only be an hour old.

If the video is freshly shot and the news story very important, the clips are sent by satellite and edited in the newsroom. When the news reporters have time, they edit the video (complete with voice-over) on location using two video recorders, picture monitors and loudspeakers. The result is then sent through as a complete news clip, electronically by satellite, or by telecom line or courier. The whole system has to cope with the speed and flexibility required by TV news programmes. It works well, but now new multimedia technologies are about to revolutionise the way news is produced.

In 1994, the chairman of Sony's Broadcast Products Company came to Europe to visit some of the major TV news studios. When chatting about the future, a senior TV executive said that what was wanted was a news editing studio in a briefcase. The chairman returned to Japan, told his staff, and a new product was born.

In July 1994, key sales, marketing, design and engineering executives from Britain, Japan and America met at Sony's annual 'product line-up' meeting. They decided to develop a completely new electronic news gathering and editing system, of which the portable editor would be a crucial part. Sony's R & D centre at Basingstoke would be responsible for developing the portable editor. A timetable was set that meant producing a working prototype for discussion with potential clients at the TV industry's main trade fair in April 1995.

The Basingstoke team agreed on a design specification to provide a highly portable, user-friendly editing studio that could marry video, sound and text to very high technical standards. It would provide 40 minutes running time on batteries, to enable editing to take place anywhere. It would be far less bulky than existing equipment, be quicker and more flexible in use, and provide a higher standard of editing. This would make the product essential equipment for all foreign and many local news reporters.

The reporter (plus camera operator) would:

1 Video the story and send the raw footage electronically to the news studio.
2 Transfer the video clips to the Sony portable editor and carry out the editing anywhere – in a hotel room, airport etc.
3 Record the voice-over, write any introductory script and send it, together with editing recommendations, through to the news studio via a modem link.

On receipt of the material the news producer could either implement the reporter's instructions directly, or make his/her own editing decisions.

Sony is the world's leading supplier of electronic news gathering equipment, with a substantial market share. So the company's experience in this market – together with its customer contacts – ensured a full understanding of the product requirements. Development engineers were able to discuss the detailed specification directly with TV news staff. For example the original design included a headphone socket in the editing computer, to enable editors to marry the sound with the pictures. Journalists and professional editors stated their preference for a small loudspeaker to allow more than one person to listen, so that was included.

The result – Sony's portable editor

Throughout the product's development, Sony benefitted from its multinational organisation. Sony's Broadcast Products Company has R & D and design development facilities in England, America and Japan. This helped the designers' understanding of how each country's TV news programmes are put together. The BBC, for instance, starts with the reporter's script, then finds pictures to illustrate the points being made. In America, the starting point is often the video and sound, around which a script is written.

With this full understanding of different customer needs, Sony was able to develop a product equally applicable in any country.

Technically, the new product incorporates three main developments:

● Digitisation – the ability to record video and sound digitally, so that it can be transferred easily to a computer; this helps the editor work faster and with more flexibility and precision.

- Compression, enabling huge quantities of information to be stored on a 3.5 inch disk (whereas ordinary floppy disks store less than two megabytes of information, the Sony portable editor uses 650 megabyte disks – developed by Sony engineers in Japan).
- A laptop computer with the power to cope with a large number of colours (invaluable when editing several pieces of colour film on the computer screen at the same time).

In addition the engineers had to write a great deal of software, including the design of a Windows-based user-friendly operating programme. This was very important, as the product had to provide all the facilities expected by professional editors plus the ease of operation required by journalists.

For Vince Harradine, principal engineer and project leader, the coordination of a project being developed in Britain and Japan required many business trips and constant communication via E-mail. For both Vince and his divisional director, David Creed, the whole project has been a terrific challenge. Both are convinced that they and their design teams have developed a world-beating multimedia product.

At the April 1995 trade fair, the portable editor was presented privately to major TV news broadcasters. The response was very positive. After further discussions, Sony's Basingstoke design centre agreed a final product proposal with colleagues in Japan. The product launch date was set for April 1996.

Of course, this is not a product that will sell millions of units. It is designed for a market niche – the world's TV newsrooms and their journalists. Yet with the market for mass products such as TVs and videos becoming ever-more competitive, Sony wants to keep ahead by adding more 'intelligence' to its products. In this case, a huge amount of value is added to the electronic components by tailoring them to the precise needs of one small segment of the electronics market. The TV stations can afford to pay the high price needed to repay Sony for the design and development work involved.

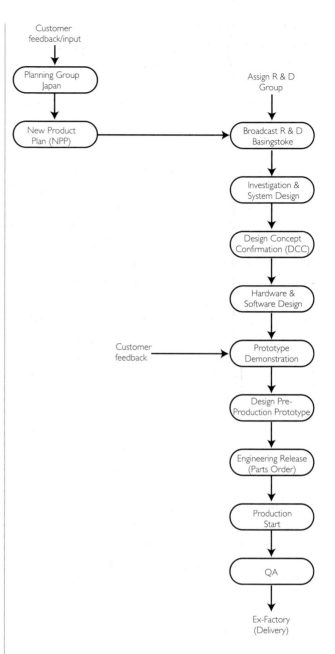

DNE-50 design flow chart

The need for teamwork

The lone inventor concept and the 'Eureka!' syndrome of product innovation are no longer applicable today, particularly as industrial engineering becomes more complex. Great design engineers like Robert Stephenson, the locomotive builder, and Isambard Kingdom Brunel, the civil engineer, possessed formidable abilities. However, with the information explosion that has occurred since their time, it is debatable whether one person is capable any longer of mastering all the specialist knowledge found in a variety of disciplines.

Teamwork is the approach adopted in today's enlightened companies who are committed to design, as being the best way to refine, develop and implement a complicated project. How should such multidisciplinary teams be organised? As David Bernstein, who runs a successful design agency, pointed out in a talk given at the London Business School, 'When a project is begun in one department and handed over to another, then inevitably some of the impetus is lost and much of the continuity and sense of ownership. The answer is frequently to create a matrix structure, a horizontal band across the vertical divisions, a project group, for example, cutting across the department divisions and consisting of members from each department.' The aim now is to change the traditional **linear** or sequential approach, where the research, design, production and marketing departments are brought in one after the other as the project progresses, to a **matrix** or teamwork approach whereby people drawn from different departments work together simultaneously on developing a project. The comparison is between running a relay race or playing in a football team.

Teamwork is vital in helping firms to maintain their competitive position. When Fuji first launched its throw-away camera, Kodak responded to the lucrative market sector which had been opened up by introducing its own disposable camera. A teamwork approach enabled Kodak to design and develop their new 'Fling' camera in record time. The company's computer-aided design system was *networked* so that all the people involved, including an outside firm of toolmakers, could work together simultaneously on the project.

Large companies organised on a **pyramidal** structure can often stifle innovation in their efforts to minimise risk. However, as James Pilditch points out in his book, *Winning Ways*, innovative

companies go to great lengths to cut through this hierarchy. At Texas Instruments they run an IDEA programme (Identify, Define, Expose, Act). Any young engineer can get $20,000 to test a new idea simply by convincing any one member of a large group of authorised technical staff that it is worth following. 'Speak'n'Spell', the voice synthesising device, was developed in this way. He goes on to add that 'The essential point is to create teams that cut across all the usual departmental walls, then to free them from the normal procedures of the company's main business.' These teams in companies such as 3M and Hewlett Packard are like small entrepreneurial start-ups which are put together to come up with new products in any way they want. They let many ideas develop, then test them quickly on the market. Basically, they are a way of getting small company vitality into an established corporation.

The dangers of poor coordination

The use of teams of people brought together from different departments to develop a new product has proved highly effective at APV Baker (formerly Baker Perkins), a heavy engineering company manufacturing machinery for baking and biscuit making. A development team might consist of members from different areas of engineering and from the sales, finance, marketing, manufacturing and industrial design departments. Such cooperation improves communication, avoiding the dangers of various departments pulling in different directions. These dangers are amusingly illustrated by Michael Smith, who runs APV Baker, in a series of diagrams on 'How not to design a swing', or 'The perils of poor coordination', quoted in Christopher Lorenz's book *The Design Dimension*.

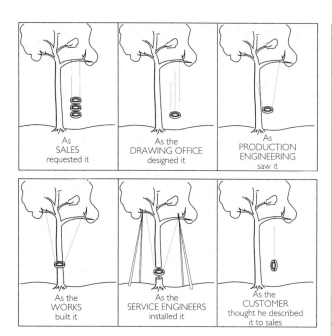

How not to design a swing

The need to shorten lead times

Olivetti used to take two years to introduce a new typewriter; now they can start to produce new designs in about two months. When IBM first introduced personal computers, they cut their normal development time from 24 months to 14 months forcing other competitors to try and follow suit. Cutting development times does not mean introducing poor products. In *A Passion for Excellence*, American authors Tom Peters and Nancy Austin describe how Xerox created a new product in 28 days that has since earned them £3 billion.

Once the decision has been taken to launch a new product, it is vitally important that the development time or **lead time** between initial design and full production is reduced as much as possible. If companies take too long to introduce a product, competitors will enter the market with similar products and erode potential profits. A study has shown that in consumer electronics, distributing a product six months late can cut life-cycle profits by

about a third. More and more businesses today are therefore trying to cut lead times, a common aim being to halve them.

Those leading companies who have succeeded in meeting this challenge have done so by cutting product introduction times to the bone, making use of **computer-aided design (CAD)** techniques. These have revolutionised the time needed to design and develop a product.

Advanced CAD facilities used in the design of products at Renishaw Plc

There are many advantages of CAD:

● Designers can create a greater variety of products. All dimensions within the design can be varied radically or by the merest fraction, as the designer wishes. The designer can sketch a basic shape for a product, produce a wire-frame model and a three-dimensional shaded model and show how all the parts used for the product are assembled together.

● The time previously spent on making models and prototypes to test the feasibility of the design can be saved, because the performance characteristics of the computer design, such as resistance to stress, can be analysed to a high degree of probability.

● The design can be modified at this early stage in the light of any problems which emerge, thus preventing the need for expensive reworking later. There is therefore a greater likelihood of the product specification being *right first time* when manufacture begins.

The need for long-term investment

The costs of developing innovative new products in high technology industries and of installing automation and robotics are so great that there is generally a long **payback period** before the investment can be expected to yield any returns. It follows from this that if UK firms wish to match the performance of aggressive overseas competitors, they may need to forgo short-term profits in order to make the long-term investments which are essential for survival.

A report on innovation for the Design Council, by Paul Gardiner and Roy Rothwell, pointed to 'the problem of British firms adopting an increasing "cash flow" view of development activity, focusing on short-term projects that yield quick results instead of taking the longer-term view and investing in innovation'. They went on to add that British firms are often at a disadvantage compared to German and Japanese firms, because of the lack of City investors who are willing to take a long-term view and lend 'patient money'. In other words, City investors generally expect a quick return and are less prepared to make investments which take years to yield any profits – the so-called 'jam today' mentality.

Private companies generally find it easier to adopt a committed policy of reinvestment than public companies, which have to explain to shareholders that their dividends are going to be lower for a few years because of money invested in developing new products. Tax policies in the UK are not very helpful either. Whereas companies can 'write off' spending on research, investment in product design and development is not allowable against tax.

The Staffordshire-based firm of JC Bamford Excavators, which manufactures earth-moving equipment, reinvests more than £20 million a year. Clearly, JCB's priorities of building up a sound operational base, rather than being concerned with short-term profits, are a lesson to other firms.

Testing stability on different gradients at JCB

Many more UK firms will need to take a long-term view in order to keep up with the competition. This is especially important if firms are to invest in new technology such as computer-aided design and manufacturing or robotics, where the pay-back period is likely to be five years or longer. In view of this, firms who are concerned only with better and better figures over the next quarter or six months are likely to find themselves being gradually squeezed out by those who *have* invested in the future.

Taking the long-term view does of course mean accepting that though a new innovation can bring in vast profits it can also fail. As Gardiner and Rothwell emphasise, 'Innovation is inherently a high-risk undertaking and one of the things we can be sure about is that there will be failures. Management must accept this and not use one failure as an excuse for withdrawing from the innovation race altogether.' It goes without saying that innovation is more likely to thrive in companies where people involved in projects that fail are not thought any less of.

The importance of research and development

The pace of innovation in today's marketplace is such that it has become vital for firms to invest heavily in **research and development (R & D)** in order to maintain their competitive edge. Firms which do not accord R & D a central role in their operations have effectively made a decision not to be in business in 10 or 15 years' time. It is within the high technology 'sunrise' industries such as computers, automobiles, electronics, pharmaceuticals and aerospace that the costs of such investment are particularly large. By the same token, however, the potential rewards, if a new product does prove to be a winner, are also much greater.

Within the automobile industry, the R & D costs for a new car can amount to around £300 million. The bill for taking a new model from design to production can be as much as £700 million. With outlays like these, car manufacturers obviously have to produce in huge volumes in order to make a profit. According to one estimate, a minimum of five million vehicles needs to be produced simply to recover the investment in R & D. Philips, the Dutch electronics group, argue that many electronics products today must capture an 8 per cent share of the world market simply to break even on R & D costs. Not surprisingly, even the largest companies find it difficult to produce in such volumes, which is why they tend to use components such as a particular engine across a number of models.

The time and level of investment required to introduce a new drug onto the market is also phenomenal. One study has estimated that on average it takes about 13 years and £85 million to take a drug from basic research to product launch. Some of this investment goes on the early 'weeding out' process. The pharmaceutical division of ICI considers approximately 10,000 new chemical compounds each year. Of these, probably no more than four will be taken into development. Only about one in ten eventually make it through the development process to reach the market. Even then, there is no guarantee of success. Inevitably, there are only a handful of drugs which are capable of generating enough profit to offset not only their own development costs but also those of the failures, as well as the 'non-starters' which never get past the development stage.

However, the rewards can be great for those companies which are successful in producing world-beating products. The anti-ulcer drug, Zantac, produced by Glaxo, the UK's leading pharmaceutical company, is a prime example. It has become the world's top selling prescription medicine, generating over £2 billion in revenues in 1993 and accounting for almost 50 per cent of the company's sales.

Within the aerospace industry, developing a new aero engine from drawing board to eventual delivery can cost as much as £2 billion. For this reason, aero engine manufacturers such as Rolls Royce are now seeking to improve and modify existing engines rather than incur the expense of designing completely new ones from scratch. For instance, their latest engine is said to have been developed at the relatively modest cost of £100 million. The development costs were reduced by taking the core of an existing engine, fitting it out with parts adapted from other units and then incorporating all the latest modifications. In addition, whereas in the past the company built as many as 39 test engines when developing a new aero engine, today eight or ten is enough as much of the early testing is done by computer simulation.

The importance according to R & D within Rolls Royce, where spending rose to a high of £253 million in 1993, has obviously been a crucial factor in explaining the company's expanding share of world markets. In the space of 10 years, Rolls Royce has increased its share from 5 per cent to the point where it now accounts for 20 per cent of civil engines made worldwide.

These examples taken from very different industries demonstrate clearly that despite the phenomenal costs, an increasing number of companies at the leading edge of technology view their commitment to research and development as an essential investment in the future.

ACTIVITY

Johnson Ceramics: designing a new product

GENERAL BACKGROUND

You work as a product designer for a design agency called First Editions and have just been consulted by a new client, Johnson Ceramics, who are based in Stoke-on-Trent, Staffordshire, and manufacture crockery. Martin Johnson, the firm's founder, has come to see you because he wants to extend the firm's product base by introducing a new range of coffee mugs. The company already has products catering for most needs, which retail through department stores, supermarkets and gift shops. However, Martin thinks there is a gap in the market for a really well-designed mug aimed at the 16–20 age group. The new coffee mug must be a good shape and size, practical to use and cheap to manufacture. It must also have a graphic design likely to appeal to this target group.

THE BRIEF

Bearing in mind the client's requirements you will need to prepare a presentation to the company, which will include a design drawing for your coffee mug, together with a written list of all the factors you took into account in planning the design which you are going to recommend to them.

The list below suggests some possible areas you will need to think about before you start designing.

1 List five questions which you would expect a short market research questionnaire to include.

2 What is the product specification for your mug?

   a) Shape: Wide or narrow? Rounded or angular? Heat loss minimised? Easy to hold? Stability? Stand to protect surfaces? Stackable when stored?

   b) Size: Capacity held? Weight when carried full? Size of handle?

   c) Materials: Made from stoneware, bone china, special glass or plastic? Resistant to what temperatures? Resistant to staining? Porosity? Expected life? Easily breakable? Microwave/dishwasher safe? Suitable for everyday or occasional use? Cost?

   d) Graphic design: On one side or both? Colours or black and white? A few colours or a riot of them? Pastels or bold primaries? Distinctiveness? Theme — landscapes, birds, flowers, cartoons, people, geometrics? Can design be extended for a whole range? Overall style geared to target group?

3 Which factors do you think are going to be most important for your brief?

4 What production methods would you advise your client to use? Mass production or craft methods? Glazed or unglazed? Interior and exterior finish? Handle fixed on or moulded in one piece?

5 Why would you make up prototypes of your design?

6 How should samples be tested?

7 How much do you think your design of coffee mug should retail for?

Information Technology

IN ASSOCIATION WITH IBM UNITED KINGDOM LIMITED

IBM

Introduction: 'solutions for a small planet'

All of us have pre-conceived ideas about the meaning of IT (information technology). Some will say it is all about computers (hardware) or floppy disks (software), while others will say it is the 'brains' behind the robot that welds motor cars together. Those involved in communications will mention a fax machine or e-mail, and if you have been taught some IT at school, you may think of spreadsheets, word-processing coursework, or perhaps using databases.

In fact, IT is more than all of these put together; providers of IT would associate themselves with the following definition: allowing tasks to be performed more quickly, more reliably, at a lower cost. It adds up to far more than the machinery, the disks, or even the robots as separate items.

IBM, which, in 1997, had a revenue of over $78 billion (making it one of the biggest companies in the world), sees IT as satisfying an overriding goal; that is, to add value to goods or services in the most efficient way in order to provide the user with a competitive advantage. The decision for most companies is no longer whether or not to install and use a particular IT application, rather which application is most likely to meet their needs.

What does IT mean?

To help your understanding of the language related to IT, the following is a summary of some of the terms used, many of which you will be familiar with.

Hardware   The machines, keyboards, monitors.

Software   The floppy discs and CD Roms which are used to store information. 'Software' also refers to the instructions which drive the machine.

EPOS (Electronic Point of Sale)   See case study on supermarkets on pages 49–52.

ISDN (Integrated Services Digital Network) Used to send large quantities of information down the telephone line at speed.

Electronic (e-) mail   A method of sending a message from one user to another (between computers). It appears on the computer screen of the receiving user. This can be likened to looking in your letterbox and collecting your mail – if you do not look, you will not find the mail!

Modem   A machine which links the computer to the telephone line and translates the electronic signal.

Facsimile (fax)   This sends a digitised image of what is on the paper, which is then printed on paper at the other end.

Database   A method of storing and retrieving large quantities of information, e.g. a list of customers, which can then be used for telephone sales or direct marketing.

Spreadsheet   A method of compiling numerical data to enable easy calculation, effective presentation and therefore understanding.

Internet   The global system, which is a publicly accessible network, allowing a vast number of computers to communicate with each other.

World Wide Web (WWW)   This allows words, pictures, video, music and other information to be sent using the Internet.

Web Page   A minute part of the World Wide Web. In order to gain access to the information on a Web page, all individual Web pages have addresses, e.g. IBM's Web page is: *www.IBM.com*

Hot-desking   The breakdown of traditional office space; from one person using the same desk, to allowing the same desk to be used by many, as and when required. As more people work from home, there is less need for a permanent desk. This maintains flexibility, whilst reducing costs for the company.

Video/Tele-conferencing   Enables several people to communicate through their computer allowing a meeting to take place, but with each member of the meeting in a different location.

CAD and **CAM**   These relate specifically to either computer-aided design or manufacture.

MRP II   For more details, see index.

1   The message which has been typed on the sender's personal computer is translated into electrical signals by the modem.
2   The message is sent to the receiver's personal computer via telephone lines.
3   The signals are translated back to words and pictures by the receiver's modem.

Electronic mail

How is IT used?

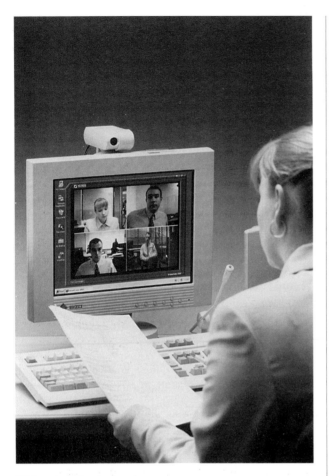

Video-conferencing
Reproduced courtesy of Daily Telegraph

ACTIVITY

For each of the following business activities, suggest the most appropriate IT application(s). Discuss the reasons for your choice within your group.

1 A company preparing cash flow forecasts required by the bank.

2 A company sending forecasts of sales volumes from the company branches to Head Office.

3 Analysing a collection of information on purchasing habits from 1990–1998.

4 Sending a message from one computer to another down the telephone line, to respond to a similar message.

5 Tracking the purchasing habits of consumers within a supermarket.

Louise Bateman, a Marketing Specialist at IBM, describes IT as being 'all-pervasive'. The following presents fictitious accounts of two people and how IT affects their lives.

A DAY IN THE LIFE OF EMMA EVANS — SALES MANAGERESS

● Stays overnight in a hotel, having made the booking by fax.

● Awoken by an alarm call which has been logged into the hotel's computer to wake her (and 54 other guests) at 6.50am.

● 7.45am–8.45am: Drives in a car to a conference using an on-board directional computer.

● 9.00am: At the conference centre, she plugs her lap-top into her mobile telephone and sends an e-mail to the head office, and then downloads three messages on to her laptop computer.

● 9.30am: Gives a presentation using IBM Lotus (Freelance Graphics) and suggests that the next meeting should be carried out via video-conferencing with a view to reducing costs to the organization, such as booking conference facilities and hotel bills.

● 3.00pm: Returns to office to consider sales forecasts on spreadsheets.

● 4.00pm: Examines newly-published database on potential customers.

● 4.30pm: Looks at the company's Web page (devoted solely to selling its products) to consider radical alteration to its design. Sales from this media have fallen in recent weeks because the company's competitors have recently put their own product information on the Web, hence reducing part of the company's competitive advantage.

● 8.15pm: Missed the tennis on television, but orders tennis items and two tickets for a musical at the West End through the laptop, using IBM's secure transaction software. She pays using VISA, although her credit card details are protected by SET (Secure Electronic Transactions) protocol.

- The next day she works at home, using the tele-networking system to e-mail her sales team to ascertain their sales figures for the week.

You might think that this person is much more likely to use computer applications in her line of work than someone who works in a warehouse. However, the next example is set in the dispatch department of a distribution company which supplies carpets and matting to various large, car-assembly plants.

A DAY IN THE LIFE OF JOSHUA JONES

- 7.30am: Arrives at work and gains access to the warehouse by swiping a smart card through a reader for identification purposes. His presence is recorded automatically for security and salary purposes.
- 7.45am: The customer, a car manufacturer, requests the daily requirements via a computer link, according to the following details:
    - the time required for assembly (normally within two hours)
    - the order in which the cars are assembled
    - the appropriate design and colours for the carpets and matting.
- A simultaneous message is sent to the lorry bay, instructing them to prepare the transport to the supplier 6 miles away.
- 7.50am: Using the warehouse computer (which is networked to all the other machines in the business), he instructs a supplier in Brazil to send more matting.
- 8.00am–8.45am: The stocks are loaded onto computerized pallets which run on tracking embedded in the warehouse floor. The rest of the day is spent meeting specific orders of this nature.
- Lunch hour: Used Radio 5 Web site to listen to broadcast of World Cup match – *www.bbc.co.uk.radio5*
- 5.00pm: On the way home from work he goes to the bank to check his balance and withdraw cash from the cash dispenser.
- 5.20pm: He goes to the supermarket where his items are scanned by laser and the cashier records these on his loyalty card.

CASE STUDY

Shopping with IT

The retail food industry is a highly competitive market and, as a consequence, companies within this sector are constantly seeking ways either to increase, or maintain, their share of the market. This is particularly true for supermarkets.

Competition has meant that there has been a narrowing of profit margins (the difference between the selling price and the cost of producing and marketing the product). Consequently, selling a larger quantity of products has become more important, which in turn requires a faster service and a greater control of costs.

Providing the best possible service to the consumer is of paramount importance. One of the major areas of concern to the consumer is convenience, which often means being able to get through the check-out as quickly as possible. Cost control and dealing with a large number of customers, all in a hurry, has led to one major application of technology – EPOS (Electronic Point of Sale). This application of technology not only brings benefits to the consumer, but also enables the supermarket to improve its communication and level of efficiency.

The check-out is a good example of the extent to which information technology has aided both the supermarket (and other retailers) as well as the consumer. In an attempt to speed up the process of passing through the check-out, all the goods are bar coded. This bar code is scanned by a laser beam which enables the automatic calculation of the bill to take place. At the same time, the scanning provides the supermarket with a wealth of data about the products that have been purchased by the consumer. The store can identify which items have been sold and, as a consequence, the present levels of stock. This, in turn, will trigger an automatic reordering procedure, either to the supermarket's own regional distribution centre, or to its suppliers.

Such a system means that the supermarket can afford to store less stock, knowing that once sales have reached a certain level, replacement stock will be delivered, arriving just in time to be placed on the shelves. This allows considerable savings in costs, as less stock needs to be stored before being placed upon the shelves. This may also provide more selling space for the supermarket to offer an even wider selection of products.

The scanning can provide vital information to the supermarket, with regard to which products are selling well, or otherwise, at all of their stores throughout the country. In addition, the company can monitor the growth of sales. This in turn can be used to help plan any changes in the marketing of the products, where they are displayed and the number of facings they are given on the shelves. They can even measure the response of consumers to any adverts or promotions that have been used, by monitoring the sales levels.

The technology has enabled the supermarkets to offer a personalized approach to their marketing. The direct contact with consumers can be achieved because of the usage of the 'reward card'. When paying for the goods, customers present their personalized card which is then 'swiped', thus relating a given customer with a particular set of purchases. This means that the company can accumulate accurate, up-to-date information on the purchasing habits of its consumers. This in turn enables the supermarket to see exactly what is bought over a period of time and whether purchasing habits are changing. It is not unusual for a given customer to receive promotional offers that match these purchasing habits through the post! Such a database can quickly highlight any changes in spending habits of one consumer, or a given group of consumers.

'Data mining' services can correlate any given elements; products that are consumed by a particular group of males, or which group of females consume a particular brand of coffee. Consequently, large retailers can, with the aid of information technology, satisfy the needs of individual customers: an essential part of marketing.

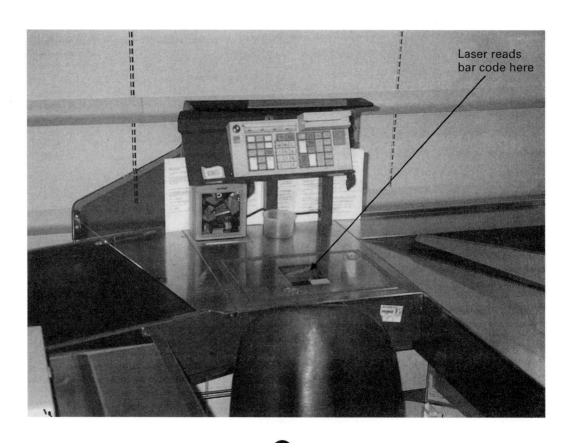

Laser reads bar code here

The targeting of the promotional material in conjunction with the supermarket's loyalty card, acts as an additional incentive for the customer to return.

Safeway have gone one step further in the utilization of technology. Satisfying the need to provide the customer with a quick and efficient service, and at the same time giving the supermarket vital information on sales, has led to the introduction of the hand gun bar code reader, 'Shop and Go'. This enables the customer to 'zap' their chosen products as they are selected from the shelves; once again the price of the selected item is automatically calculated and the sale is recorded for stock replacement purposes. On reaching the check-out, the total cost of the products purchased has been calculated and payment is made in the normal way.

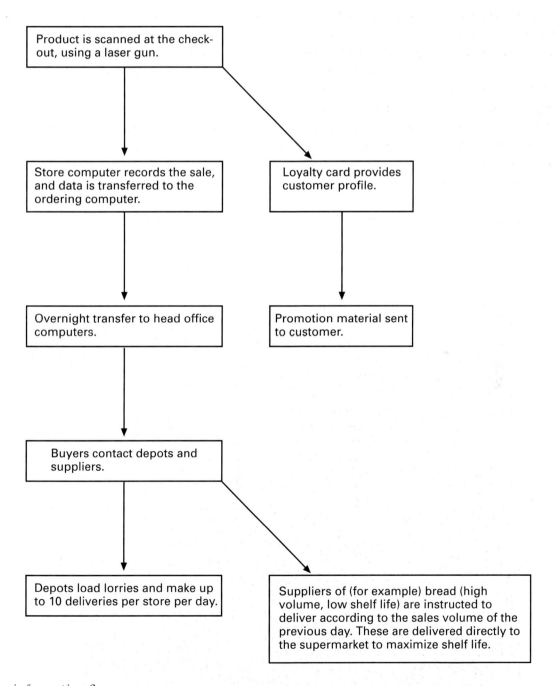

How the information flows . . .

Random checks are made to ensure that all items within the customer's trolley have been either scanned or scanned properly. Such a process is another method to enhance the experience of shopping in an attempt to eradicate what is thought to be the main area of concern to customers: their dread of the check-out queue!

Shop and Go with IT
Reproduced by kind permission of Safeway Plc

Information technology has provided an acceptable solution to a given problem, whilst at the same time enabling additional benefits to be available to all concerned.

 DISCUSSION POINTS

1 How might a farmer make use of IT?

2 What are the costs and benefits for a supplier of goods to a supermarket which uses EPOS?

What are the limitations of IT?

Although IT may be seen as the solution to all our problems, implementing any form of IT application may have its drawbacks:

1 **The danger of over-reliance**   When documents are held within a particular file/machine/network there is a possibility of the system 'crashing'. As a consequence, material may be lost, sometimes permanently. This is why it is so important to take a regular copy of your computer data to store in a safe place as a back-up. In a similar way (for example when airline bookings are taken using a computer), a computer crash can result in some very disappointed customers.

2 **Objectivity**   Although computer systems have been built to allow for changes in variables, there is always a need for human intuition and creative input.

3 **Human attitude to technology and change**   Certain individuals tend not to accept a change in technology and therefore resent having to use computers/IT, fearing, for example, the possibility of job losses.

4 **Set-up and running costs**   The significant level of capital investment needed to purchase the hardware and the specialized help which is always needed to train computer users and maintain the computers in working condition, may be prohibitive for many small businesses.

5 **The millennium timebomb**   The systems within most computers have been designed without this issue in mind, i.e. the computer will not recognize the date 2000. Computers recognize the date by reading the last two digits, e.g. 1998 would be read as 98, therefore, when the year becomes 2000, the date will be read as 00, i.e. 1900! It is feared that literally thousands of computers might crash on 1 January 2000. The Government has been heavily criticized for its lack of foresight in tackling this problem and its reluctance to provide finance for the hiring of consultants who may be able to find a solution. In October 1997, Barbara Roche, the DTI minister responsible for IT, announced the introduction of an Action 2000 unit to help solve the 'timebomb' problem.

The future of IT

Given the frantic rate of change which has been observed in IT over recent years, it is very difficult to predict the changes which are likely to be seen during the twenty-first century. However, such a prediction may well include the following:

- Intelligent materials, e.g. food packaging that includes sensors to detect changing temperatures, or a signal to indicate that the food is unsafe to eat.
- Cheap, sensitive sensors for road tolls (for example), which are likely to become a reality in the very near future for most town centres.
- Electronic business (e-business) – shopping from home via the Internet, which is already done by supermarkets such as Tesco, or banking from home using a personal computer. First Direct have recently launched one of the first on-line banking services. Consumers benefit because of the convenience and companies are likely to benefit because they will no longer need expensive town centre stores and paper catalogues.
- Virtual Reality – supermarket companies are already using this facility to design and assess shelf displays, which are then tested on consumers using a headset and a virtual store. Perhaps a logical progression of this formidable tool is Virtual Shopping? (Source: *The Grocer*, 8 February 1997.)
- Interactive kiosks, where people can use smart cards and payment mechanisms to perform a range of personal and business transactions, e.g. purchasing train tickets, reading entertainment listings, booking holidays.
- Web TV – consumers who fear using a computer keyboard are more at home with a remote control used with a TV set. Access to the Internet will be achieved through a TV set 'top box', which will later be incorporated into the TV itself. This will allow simple Internet searches to be made and will bring the cost of access within easy reach of most households.
- The fear of the computer keyboard will be further diminished with the use of voice activation, and later voice response, technology.
- Wirelessness – devices may no longer need a cable, allowing greater flexibility for the use of hardware, and, as a consequence, meaning that people can work at home, at the office or on the train, using more applications.
- Small businesses are able to take advantage of IT, as e-business takes no heed of the size of a business. This may well allow small companies to develop new, bright ideas and exploit competitive advantages over larger rivals.

Companies will need to change their working practices to encompass IT as an all-pervasive medium of the commercial world. Plenty of companies have a Web page, although as yet, few use the Internet creatively to reach new markets. There is also the likelihood that the organization structure may change as IT requires different skills. Clare Birks, Corporate Affairs Manager at IBM, suggests that such changes are readily welcomed by senior management and front-line workers, although they can be resisted by middle managers.

Only once citizens are comfortable with the use of IT will smart cards (e.g. for personal transactions) become more acceptable. This will, in turn, depend on people becoming familiar with them. This catch-22 scenario needs to be addressed by the Government, who will surely benefit as some of its departments will be able to perform transactions with citizens, e.g. road tax (through the Department of Transport) and income tax payment (through the Inland Revenue).

The Government has so far allowed the competitive private sector to lead the way in terms of development programmes, especially those that utilize smart cards. It can be argued that such a decision has been driven by the possibility that civil-rights activists may object to the further advancement of IT leading to the infringement on one's freedom. Smart cards are used for market research and there may be a time when the information is transferred on customer's buying habits, without the customer knowing.

IBM is committed to such developments and is one of the companies at the forefront with its programme of research. The potential is infinite; as we are given more ways to communicate across the Internet, it will become the natural way to communicate and run businesses. As Marcus East of IBM puts it, 'This is not the future of IT, but the future of business enabled by IT.'

Production

Introduction: the role of production

By definition, manufacturing firms exist to manufacture or make a product. It is the value added by firms during the production process which enables them to sell their finished product at a much higher price than the pure cost of the raw materials used in their manufacture. For example, car tyres sell for far more than the rubber that they are made from, furniture for far more than the cost of the timber alone.

In order to increase the amount of value added, firms need to make the best possible decisions in four key areas of production: **scale**, **method**, **quality** and **location**.

In addition, they are continually striving to improve efficiency and productivity, in order to survive in a climate of increasing overseas competition.

Are firms getting bigger?

There is a growing trend, both within individual industries and in terms of total manufacturing output within the UK, for production to be concentrated more and more into the hands of a few large firms. The 100 largest manufacturing companies employ roughly one third of the labour force and account for approximately 35 per cent of total net output.

Firms can grow in size by means of:

- **Organic growth** Firms expand by taking on more employees, investing in more machinery, buildings and so on.
- **Acquisitions or mergers** Firms expand by joining together to form a single, larger organisation.

The trend towards concentration of production into a smaller number of firms has been mainly due to the increase in the number of mergers. In recent years, most mergers have been conglomerate mergers, where firms in different industries have joined together, diversifying their product base. This avoids the risks inherent in limiting their operations to a narrow range of products in one industry – that is, the dangers of putting 'all their eggs in one basket'.

However, the diversification process can be taken too far if firms expand into many unrelated industries in which they have no expertise. The only answer may then be to sell some of their fringe activities and concentrate on those they define as core activities, a process which can prove very lucrative.

Overall, this trend towards larger firms can be attributed to the cost savings which result from an increase in the scale of production.

Scale of production

Large firms are able to produce their goods at a more competitive price than small firms because their fixed costs are spread over the larger number of units which are produced.

Once gained, this competitive edge becomes self-perpetuating, enabling large firms to expand their market share still further. Smaller firms cannot afford the initial outlay which makes these savings possible, and therefore are unable to operate as cost effectively. They can only survive by producing for a specialised area of the market. Rolls Royce does this in the car market where its 0.1 per cent market share is dwarfed by the big four UK manufacturers: Rover (31.6 per cent), Vauxhall (19.5 per cent), Ford (18.9 per cent) and Nissan (13.8 per cent).

As firms get bigger they gain the benefits of being able to spread costs and make savings by operating more efficiently. These are known as **economies of scale**. Apart from the **internal** economies of scale (see Table 5.1) possible within the firm, there are also **external** economies which can result from firms grouping together, such as:

● The presence of component suppliers nearby.

TABLE 5.1 *Internal economies of scale*

Type of economy	Enables large firms to:
Purchasing	Buy materials more cheaply by taking advantage of bulk discounts.
	Employ trained buyers who can negotiate the best deals.
Production	Use mass-production techniques to speed up and increase production.
	Afford to buy large, specialised, technically advanced machinery.
	Use specialised division of labour.
Risk-bearing	Afford to take more risks with launching a new product, as with a diversified range of products they always have others to fall back on if one fails.
	Afford to employ an R & D department.
Financial	Borrow more easily as they have greater reserves and are perceived as being more creditworthy by lenders.
	Obtain loans at more favourable rates of interest.
	Afford to use the services of accountants and other financial advisers.
Marketing	Afford to advertise extensively, as the additional cost per unit produced is small when spread over a large output.
	Afford to employ specialist sales and after-sales staff and run advertising departments.
Administrative	Sustain high overheads spread over greater output.
	Afford the higher salary packages necessary to recruit the best managers.
	Afford to install sophisticated computerised systems for controlling and monitoring the business.

- The use of one firm's end product or even its waste as raw material for another firm.
- The existence of a skilled, experienced workforce – perhaps trained at a specialised local college.

Of course, an increase in the scale of operations does not lead solely to benefits such as cost reductions and improvements in efficiency. It can also lead to **diseconomies of scale**, such as excessive **bureaucracy**. Companies can be stifled by the red tape involved in large company record-keeping, communications and committee decision making. Big, unwieldy firms often lose their capacity to innovate and become unable to respond to changes in the market.

To overcome these problems, the majority of large firms now split their organisations into smaller divisions, which function independently on a day-to-day basis yet remain within the overall control of the parent company. They therefore operate, in effect, as smaller firms.

Method of production

The decision as to which production method a firm should adopt is influenced by several factors:

- The nature and variety of the products.
- Market factors such as the size and frequency of orders.
- The stage of development reached by the firm.

At one end of the scale is **job production**, based on 'one-offs' or small orders, often of luxury goods. This can be carried out on a small scale, as with custom-made clothes, or on a large scale, as with shipbuilding and aircraft manufacture. This type of production is **labour intensive**, either because a skilled workforce is required due to the nature of the work, or because the volume of production is too low for any major investment in machinery to be justified. It is the method most often used by start-up businesses.

Once demand increases and the design of the product is capable of being simplified and replicated to a certain standard, then it becomes both economically worthwhile and technically feasible for

mass production techniques to be employed. Mass production involves making large volumes of identical products to the same standard, at a low unit cost. Products can be mass produced in batches or as a continuous flow.

The second type, **batch production,** is a more efficient method than job production as the work process is divided into its component operations. Each operation is completed for the whole batch of items being produced before the next operation is carried out. Batch production accounts for 75 per cent to 85 per cent of total production in western countries.

The third type, **flow production**, is the most efficient method of all. Once the work on one operation is completed, the items are passed as a continuous flow to the next stage without having to wait for a batch to be completed. This is very **capital intensive** because an automated production line requires a heavy initial outlay. As labour costs per unit are minimised, however, variable costs per unit are kept low.

The degree of job specialisation involved in flow-production processes creates a highly defined division of labour. This can result in high productivity, though the boredom of the job may lead quality to slip. The modern approach is to avoid the repetition involved in a high division of labour. (See Table 5.2 on page 57 for more details about each method of production.)

The modern approach to production

Today, most manufacturing companies focus upon two main strategies: **lean production** and **total quality management**, both of which have come from successful and influential Japanese companies such as Toyota and Sony. British firms had previously thought that the Japanese approach could only work with super-dedicated Japanese workers, but that view had to change when Sony, Nissan, Toyota and many others set up successful factories in Britain, using British workers.

Lean production

Prompted by shortages after defeat in the Second World War, Japanese companies had to be very resourceful in their approach to business. In the absence of any plastics industry in Japan, Sony's first tape recorders used tape made from paper, and Toyota, while in its early years as a car producer, had to find ways of manufacturing with the minimum possible machinery and materials. By 1950, Toyota had only produced 2,685 cars in its history, while a single American Ford factory made 7,000 cars a day.

The American mass production system used a series of huge machines, each dedicated to one task. One would press metal into the shape of a front bumper, another into a back bumper, another would produce the wing and so on. As reported by Jim Womack, Dan Jones and Dan Roos in their book, *The Machine That Changed The World*, 'The massive and expensive western press lines were designed to operate at about 12 strokes a minute to make a million or more of a given part in a year.' In order to compete, Toyota realised they would have to find ways of producing cheaply without the advantage of the Americans' huge scale of production.

The solution was to design machines that could be used for many different operations. The problem was the length of time taken to reset the machines. At first it took a whole day to change a stamping machine from producing one part to making another. By the late 1950s, however, Toyota engineers had reduced this time to just three minutes, and had so simplified the process that factory line workers could do it without needing help from engineers. This carried with it the advantage of flexibility. If buying habits changed in America, Ford could not react quickly, because each production line was dedicated to producing a particular product in a particular way. Toyota's multi-purpose machines could adapt quickly to a surge of demand for open-top cars or right-hand drive models.

JUST IN TIME

The same desire to minimise the use of resources also led to Toyota's most famous discovery – just in time (JIT). To reduce the space occupied, and money tied up, by high buffer stocks of materials and work in progress, Toyota devised a card ordering system known as kanban. The rule was that no components would be made, or supplies ordered, unless the instruction was given by the kanban. If an assembly worker fitted eight left-hand car doors, a kanban would be sent to the door production team which would produce another batch of eight. In theory these would arrive just in time before the assembly worker's remaining stock ran out.

At first, the new system caused chaos, as parts arrived late and suppliers complained about making frequent deliveries of small batches. Yet Toyota soon realised that the knife-edged nature of this system was its very strength. If a faulty batch of components to the door production team caused a halt to the final assembly line, the supplier was soon threatened with quality improvements or paying for the lost output. Existing with only an hour's worth of buffer stock ensured that every production, supply or quality fault would be acted on quickly, or else be clear for all to see. By 1990, Toyota was producing over four million cars a year, far outstripping any European or Japanese producer and rivalling the American giants, Ford and General Motors.

JIT also has enormous implications for managing the workforce. High stock levels were the management cushion against workforce indiscipline, be it absenteeism or strike action. Now a strike might shut the factory down within an hour or two. Accordingly, it becomes essential that management encourage cooperation instead of confrontation. Factory workers need to be treated as valued members of a complete team – trusted, trained and consulted.

As a result, JIT leads firms to rethink their approach to factory work. The traditional approach of splitting work into repetitive fragments results in an uncooperative workforce. So firms organise the workforce into teams, working together on large units of work instead of working in isolation on the same boring task.

From its origins at Toyota, this approach has spread widely throughout the west. In Britain, firms such as Rover, IBM and Rolls Royce have adopted and adapted JIT to suit their own needs. Rolls Royce has divided its car plant into 16 zones, each acting as a business within a business, responsible for purchasing, cost, quality and delivery. The engine assembly team, for example, has three hours to assemble each engine, and is then responsible for testing it. Rolls Royce's new approach has halved the break-even level from 2,800 cars per year to 1,400.

Total quality

Linked to lean production is the desire for zero defects, in other words a fault-free system. This is needed to avoid wasting time and money, rectifying faults and to ensure maximum customer satisfaction and therefore repeat purchase. The high cost of poor quality was shown by an analysis of British banks by the American quality consultant, Philip Crosby Inc. It showed that British banks waste more than 50 per cent of their operating costs because of error-prone procedures that result in problems such as lost documents.

The management of quality can be approached in three main ways:

- Total quality management (TQM) is the acceptance by every member of an organisation that quality is his or her primary duty, whether dealing with a colleague or a customer. This often requires a huge change in management and staff attitudes.
- The lean production approach is to focus the quality effort upon eliminating defects in every stage of the design, manufacturing and delivery.
- Quality assurance systems such as BS 5750 aim to provide guaranteed levels of quality; then customers can decide whether the promised quality level meets their requirements.

TOTAL QUALITY MANAGEMENT

The first European companies to adopt TQM methods were those facing the fiercest competition from Japan, such as Rank Xerox and Philips. Both started by adopting Japanese ideas such as quality circles, but found that quality improvements only became significant once senior management made quality a priority throughout the business. Philips started to measure quality in terms of defects per million, in imitation of the Japanese. This had real impact, because once departments were made aware of their quality shortfalls, they started to discuss how to improve. Defect levels fell by a factor of 100 and Philips' exports to Japan doubled in 10 years.

In a recent survey, the chief executives of 230 top European companies believed that their companies' gross profit margins could be boosted by 17 per cent and variable costs cut by 35 per cent if TQM practices were widely employed.

LEAN APPROACH TO QUALITY

Many firms suspect that TQM has become over-sold by management consultants, and that its attempt to change attitudes can radically backfire. So they approach the pursuit of better quality as part of the lean production process, often helped by the use of continuous improvement (or kaizen) groups. These meeting groups of shop-floor workers, supervisors and, often, engineers attempt to come up with new ideas regularly, to improve efficiency, quality and working conditions on the factory floor.

The traditional management approach was to send in consultants every five years to recommend a complete overhaul of production. Kaizen looks to a whole series of small changes recommended by the workforce, to provide continuous and therefore less threatening change. This approach has been helpful for the Japanese producer of excavators, Komatsu, in the north-east of England and for the motor spares company, Unipart.

BS 5750 – QUALITY ASSURANCE

The main criticism of BS 5750 is that it is not a way of improving quality, only of proving your level of quality. In other words, a producer could obtain the BS 5750 award for promising that its supplies will have a 10 per cent defect rate. This may be a harsh criticism as it at least gives the customer a clear basis for judging one supplier against another. In that way it encourages firms to work at improving quality standards.

Another criticism of BS 5750 (and its worldwide counterpart ISO 9002) is that it is overly bureaucratic. To gain the award you must be able to show the paperwork evidence for everything you do. In that way the customer can be sure that, no matter who is on holiday, the production process will be carried out in exactly the same way as usual.

Despite the doubts, British Airways are among many firms to have benefited from adopting BS 5750. The standards led to the discovery that, among other problems, baggage handlers were not trained to cope with new, automated unloading methods. Now workers are updated whenever changes occur. In the first year, complaints dropped by 65 per cent and the time spent fixing problems by 60 per cent.

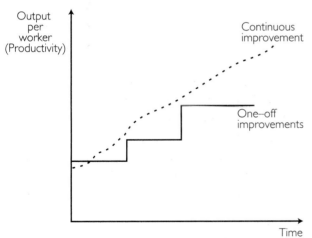

Kaizen: continuous improvement

Allied Domecq plc – Who put the hole in the donut?

Allied Domecq plc is a major international drinks brand and retailing group with an annual turnover in excess of £4.3 billion. The group which is publicly quoted on the London, Amsterdam and Brussels Stock Exchanges is focused into two main business areas: Spirits & Wine and Retailing. Together they produce approximately 60% and 40% of group profits respectively. Its spirits brands include Beefeater Gin, Teacher's, Ballantine's and Canadian Club whiskies, Courvoisier and Tequila Sauza. In retailing, the group operates some 4,000 pubs in the UK and is the world leader in food franchising through the US based businesses of Dunkin' Donuts and Baskin Robbins.

The group employs more than 50,000 people worldwide and aims to provide outstanding customer service. To ensure that its wide range of spirit and retail brands meets customer and consumer demands the company has developed an extensive network of either wholly owned, joint venture, third party operations and franchised outlets around the world.

On the retailing side, Allied Domecq plc is the world No. 4 in retailing ranked by the number of outlets, with over 14,000 in over 60 countries, handling 30 million retail transactions weekly. These range from US franchised food products such as Dunkin' Donuts, Baskin Robbins ice-cream and Togo's sandwiches worldwide, to the meals and drinks served in the 3,700 pubs in the UK.

Allied Domecq not only creates employment and generates wealth but also provides another ingredient vital to a successful society – enjoyment. The group publishes a comprehensive list of its products and services on its website which is listed as: **http://www.allieddomecqplc.com**

ACTIVITY

Using the Allied Domecq website, find the answers to the following questions about Allied Domecq products.

1 How many donuts are sold by Dunkin' Donuts each day?

2 Where was the first Togo's eatery located?

3 How many people does Baskin Robbins serve each week?

4 What is a 'firkin'?

5 In Japan how many bottles of Ballantine's 30 Years Old Scotch Whisky is equal to the price of a small Nissan car?

6 Who put the hole in the donut?

Location of production

What factors do firms consider when deciding where to locate? The eventual choice is usually based on a combination of factors, including the presence of raw materials, markets, transport, labour, government grants and the characteristics of the site.

In theory, the decision should be made by weighing up the fixed and variable costs of operating on each available site and comparing them with the expected revenues. However, it is becoming recognised that decisions are not always made on such rational, financial grounds. One of the first Japanese firms to set up a factory in Britain was Nittan, a manufacturer of smoke detectors. When the Japanese managing director arrived to search for a site in 1970, he decided on Old Woking in Surrey because it was close to Heathrow airport, near to the company's bank in the City and had excellent golf courses nearby! Larger firms, investing many hundreds of millions, are more likely to apply more scientific criteria.

RAW MATERIALS

These can be minerals like iron and coal or, more commonly today, components, which may be the semi-processed or finished products of other firms. In the past, poor transport facilities made this a vital factor, so steelworks were established near coalfields. Supplies of materials still influence location today if the materials are:

● Bulk reducing, as in the sugar refining industry. Sugar loses seven eighths of its weight when processed, so it is uneconomic to transport bulky, raw sugar beet for long distances. This is why the factories are located in the growing areas like East Anglia.
● Perishable, as in the fruit canning industry.

MARKETS

As the pull of raw materials has declined with the improvement of transport links, nearness to markets has become increasingly important. This is especially true of:

● Bulk increasing (weight gaining) processes such as bottling or canning drinks. Coca-Cola, for example, have bottling plants close to most centres of population. It is not worth transporting bottles over long distances when the water can be just as easily added to the syrup near to the marketplace.
● Perishable items such as bread, which must quickly reach the customer.

TRANSPORT

For firms with national and, even more, international markets, speed of access to motorways, ports and railways is of great importance. Not only because time is money, but also because customers expect deliveries to be made exactly when requested. Delays due to traffic jams are no longer acceptable in an era of just in time production. Today, more than 90 per cent of deliveries take place by road. Perhaps this will change in future, as the Channel Tunnel and ever-higher taxes on petrol encourage greater use of the railways.

LABOUR

There are two ways in which firms may look at their labour requirements. If the production process is labour intensive, low wage rates may be a key location factor. So the choice is likely to be an area of traditionally high unemployment. In many other cases, the firm will be more concerned to obtain (or keep) workers and managers with the right skills. Hence computer software companies tend to favour the Thames Valley area, while electronics manufacturers go to Scotland's 'Silicon Glen'.

CHARACTERISTICS OF THE SITE

Large plants like oil refineries and steel works require vast amounts of flat, cheap land. Nearness to water for cooling is often important. Over half of Scotland's whisky distilleries are sited around the Moray Firth, where the best water, which has drained through peat, is found.

For service businesses, the key site characteristics are passing traffic (on foot or by car), ease of parking and the availability of sites of the right size.

GOVERNMENT INTERVENTION

Successive governments have adopted regional policies in order to redistribute wealth and employment more evenly and halt migration to the south east. Expansion in the prosperous areas can be controlled by restricting planning permission for new houses or factories. At the same time relocation to the **Assisted Areas** has been encouraged by offering incentives such as a 15 per cent grant towards capital expenditure on plant machinery and buildings. More significant has been the government's use of **Regional Selective Assistance**. This has been used to attract foreign firms considering Britain among other possible European sites. In 1994, the Korean firm Samsung was persuaded to build its first European factory in Britain. It is hoped that if Samsung is as successful here as Japanese firms have been, then other Korean firms will come to Britain as well.

WHY DO FIRMS TEND TO REMAIN IN THE SAME LOCATION?

Once an industry has become established in an area, it will often stay even when the original location advantages have disappeared. This **industrial inertia** occurs for many reasons. The investment in fixed assets – buildings and machinery – may be great; even more important are the skills and knowledge of the labour force. To move away would be likely to cause the break-up of what is often a company's greatest asset – its people. In any case, completely new **green-field** sites are difficult and expensive to set up because of the additional infrastructure needed, such as the roads and services which have to be provided.

Many firms are loyal to the area in which they were founded, but others have become **footloose**, or willing to move anywhere if the incentives are great enough. Mercedes Benz have considered setting up a car plant outside Germany and Jaguar cars have considered America. In 1993, Timex was willing to close down its Dundee plant and move production overseas. The firm had been established in Dundee for 40 years, yet its American parent company felt no underlying loyalty to the area.

The impact of automation

What constitutes efficient production? Most firms would say that to reduce costs and improve quality would be a sure-fire way of beating rivals and ensuring commercial success. Important as they are, though, to get these factors right is still only part of the answer. Increasingly, in the current climate of over-capacity, worldwide competition and rapid technological change, firms must also be able to compete on factors other than price or quality. They must offer a much wider range of products, by being able to adapt their production process quickly in response to changing market demands and by reducing lead times – the time taken to develop a new product until it is ready for full production.

The widespread automation of production processes which has been advocated in recent years is no longer seen as a universal solution for industry's problems.

There is no shortage of examples illustrating the benefits of automation. In addition, more advanced robots are continually being developed. For example, Ford developed the world's first 'seeing' robot. A magnet mounted on the robot's arm collects an engine part such as a crankshaft from storage. The robot identifies it by 'seeing' the part's shape and comparing it to information stored in a memory bank. The part is then placed with pinpoint accuracy on the production line.

However, unless the design and organisation of the production line are simplified and streamlined beforehand, automation will merely accentuate the existing problems, not solve them. Nothing less than the complete reorganisation of the whole production line will work, as the introduction of automation on its own merely speeds up an existing inefficient process and adds the purchase and upkeep of the machinery as an extra cost burden.

CASE STUDY

The National Grid Company plc

W̲e own and operate the motorways of power – the high voltage electricity transmission system in England and Wales. We take the electricity produced by the generators and transport it across our network of overhead lines and underground cables to your local electricity supplier and to some large industrial users.

Electricity is usually generated in power stations at 25,000 volts, then increased by substation transformers to 275,000 and 400,000 volts and fed into the national grid system to be transmitted, efficiently, over long distances. Some large industrial customers requiring large amounts of electricity may be supplied direct from substations. The supply will be reduced for distribution to towns, villages and direct to small industrial customers. Regional electricity companies distribute electricity at lower voltages through local networks into homes and businesses.

The National Grid plays an essential part in the lives of everyone living in England and Wales. Each time you switch on your television set, turn on the lights at work or walk home at night with the help of street lights, you rely on electricity which has passed across the high voltage transmission network.

Unlike other forms of energy, electricity cannot be stored in large quantities. As it is needed it must be generated, as it is generated it must be used. National Grid has to match demand with the generation capacity of power stations (principally fuelled by coal, gas, oil and nuclear) – minute by minute, 24 hours a day, 365 days a year. Adverse weather conditions and major or local events can affect the demand for electricity. The national grid is kept in operation at all times and in all weathers to ensure that electricity is supplied where it is needed, when it is wanted.

Demand varies according to the time of day, time of year and weather conditions, but peaks can be anticipated in advance and sufficient extra generating capacity made available to meet them. Popular TV programmes can lead to sudden increases in electricity demand, known as 'TV pickups'. These result from viewers turning on lights, kettles, electric blankets etc., when programmes end.

Under the Electricity Act 1989, the National Grid Company has a duty to develop and maintain an efficient, co-ordinated and economical system of electricity transmission and to facilitate competition in the supply and demand of that electricity. However, it also has to have a regard to the preservation of amenity. To fulfil these requirements, economic, operational and environmental factors must be considered when assessing the relative merits of overhead lines or underground cable.

Overhead lines

- Have a visual impact on the landscape – substantial structures
- Pylons impracticable in dense, urban areas
- Construction quicker (five times as fast)
- Repairs less disruptive
- Less costly

Underground cables

- Impact on the landscape during construction
- Can disturb flora and fauna / archaeological sites
- Can cause restrictions on land use
- Cable laying requires more trenches / wider concrete bays
- Repair may take 25 times longer
- Costs 15–25 times as much to install

There are constraints on farming operations from both.

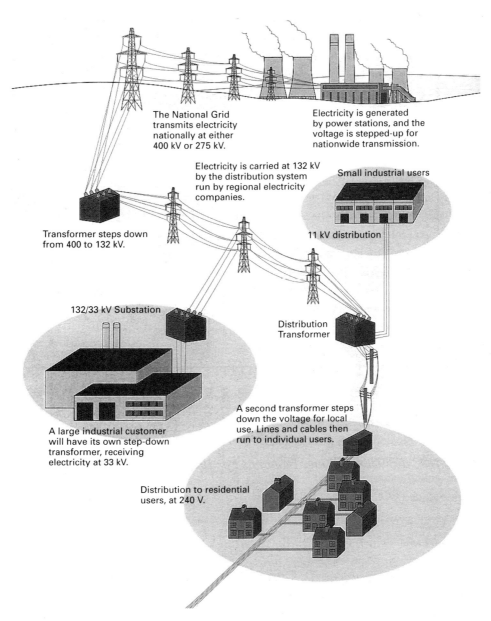

The National Grid transmits electricity nationally at either 400 kV or 275 kV.

Electricity is generated by power stations, and the voltage is stepped-up for nationwide transmission.

Electricity is carried at 132 kV by the distribution system run by regional electricity companies.

Small industrial users

Transformer steps down from 400 to 132 kV.

11 kV distribution

132/33 kV Substation

Distribution Transformer

A large industrial customer will have its own step-down transformer, receiving electricity at 33 kV.

A second transformer steps down the voltage for local use. Lines and cables then run to individual users.

Distribution to residential users, at 240 V.

Generation, transmission and distribution of electricity

correct output which workers should achieve in a day could be decided on. Workers who then met this productivity target should be paid much higher wages.

Though his principles later became widely adopted as the basis of **work study** methods, he was severely criticised, even in his own time, for seeing money as the main motivating factor and for reducing workers to the level of efficient machines. In all fairness, however, few employers have been willing to implement all his ideas fully, like having no limit to the amount highly productive workers can earn.

E MAYO (1933)

Mayo's research has been influential in revealing that the general ethos and values held by informal social groups at work are more important in determining productivity levels than are other changes.

In the famous Hawthorne experiment, a group of workers were segregated in order to observe the effect on output and morale of various changes to their working environment. As each improvement was introduced, such as incentive payments, rest pauses, shorter hours and refreshments, productivity rose. Then it was decided to return to the original conditions of a six-day, 48-hour week, with no incentives, no rest pauses and no refreshments. Expecting a fall in output, researchers were amazed when productivity soared to the highest levels ever reached!

Though it seemed a mystery then, Mayo's later explanation was that by this time a tightly knit social group had formed, who benefited from the attention shown by researchers and who worked to achieve the output levels they thought the researchers expected. The research has stimulated an increasing tendency for production to be organised in small groups and encouraged managers to realise the importance of praise, attention and good communications in getting workers to identify and work towards company goals.

AH MASLOW (1943)

Maslow argued that people seek to satisfy a hierarchy of needs, with lower-level needs being satisfied before higher-level needs (see the diagram on page 12). With increased living standards this century, lower-level needs such as those for physical survival and safety tend to have been satisfied. Firms who now wish to persuade their employees to work harder can only do so by offering them the opportunity to fulfil higher-level needs. These include the satisfaction of social needs (belonging to a group), esteem needs (being highly regarded) and the need for self-fulfilment (gaining satisfaction by being creative, for instance).

D MCGREGOR (1960)

Theories like Taylor's, which view employees as disliking work and which emphasise high wages and strict supervision as the best way of ensuring maximum productivity, are based on certain assumptions about what workers are like. McGregor called these assumptions *Theory X*. Instead, his own *Theory Y* is based on assumptions that people find work natural, that they exercise self-control in meeting objectives to which they are committed, that they will not only accept but actively seek responsibility and will want to take part in decision making.

The implications of McGregor's theories are far-reaching. Clearly, firms need to create Theory Y climates and working conditions so that workers can motivate themselves, with managers performing a supportive role rather than a traditional controlling role.

F HERZBERG (1966)

Herzberg developed his theory of incentives by asking a sample of employees what made them happy or unhappy at work. On this basis, he identified *hygiene* or *maintenance factors*, such as adequate pay and working conditions, as not being **motivators**. If these are inadequate, workers will fight to have them improved, but they do not actually encourage people to work harder. The *real* motivators were factors relating to the job itself, like the opportunity for achievement, recognition and advancement. The chance to exercise creativity and take on responsibility were also important.

Contrary to Taylor's early ideas, these later writers have argued that people are motivated by many needs and do not work for money alone. In fact, it can often be seen that people's whole identity stems from the work they do and the organisation they work for. The evidence that work is a psychological need is borne out by the effects of unemployment on people, many of whom report a loss of identity and esteem and a general feeling of alienation from society.

ACTIVITY

The needs fulfilled by different jobs

1 Identify which higher-order needs, such as the need for esteem and recognition, or for self-fulfilment through the chance to exercise creativity or take on responsibility, are likely to be fulfilled in the following jobs:

- Rock star
- Barrister
- Surgeon
- Cabinet minister
- First division footballer
- Train driver
- Airline pilot
- Music composer
- Fashion designer

2 Which needs would you expect your future job to fulfil?

 DISCUSSION POINT

Do you think unemployed people suffer through not being able to fulfil any of these needs through a job?

CASE STUDY

Eurostar and the graduate engineer

Even though the Channel Tunnel started with teething problems, the Eurostar train service between London and Paris has been a great success. It has already grabbed a 40 per cent share of the London-Paris market, to the discomfort of British Airways and Air France. A great attraction of the Eurostar is its smooth, comfortable ride – ideal for tourists and business travellers. The train was designed and built jointly in France and Britain by GEC ALSTHOM.

Stephen Stretch, a young graduate engineer, made his own contribution. Based in Birmingham, he works for the British arm of GEC ALSTHOM, a joint venture owned equally by Britain's GEC and France's Alcatel Alsthom.

The modern approach to graduate recruitment is to provide challenges, not just training. When Stephen took a summer vacation job at GEC ALSTHOM, he was given the chance to spend some time at the Eurostar test facility. This tests the train's electrical power and control systems through a simulation of the complete London-Paris journey. Stephen was testing and fault finding the electrical systems as the train design was being developed.

Sponsored by GEC through his second and third years at Sheffield University, Stephen received a First Class Honours degree and was given a place on the GEC ALSTHOM graduate trainee scheme. The programme focuses as much on the personal skills of the trainees as on their product knowledge. Stephen's problem solving, teamwork and communication skills were developed by a tough outward bound course. This was followed by a series of projects to be completed during his 18 months of training in the main sections of the company. Stephen also took French lessons, which led to two weeks' training at a French GEC ALSTHOM site.

With the training completed successfully, Stephen is now an assistant electrical engineer. He is part of a team designing and developing the trains for a new rail link between Stockholm city centre and the neighbouring airport. The seven, four-carriage trains for this new line represent a multimillion pound contract that will take approximately four years to complete and employ many hundreds of people.

Stephen's role involves:

- Calculating and designing some of the electrical requirements for the trains.
- Meeting and discussing equipment requirements with suppliers.
- Monitoring the designs provided by electrical suppliers (including power supplies, lighting, heating systems and much more).
- Constantly looking for new and better ways to build a train.

For GEC ALSTHOM, the Swedish order is a relatively small one. Bigger contracts, such as the London Underground's Jubilee and Northern lines, involve hundreds of train carriages. Part of the job of engineers is to decide on the most efficient production method. Stephen expects that his trains will be produced in the traditional way – the so-called static build. In other words, each carriage is assembled in one place. For the huge London Underground orders, the company is making its first ever move towards flow production: each carriage will be assembled in stages, then moved on to the next production stage in the equivalent of a car production line.

The engineering decisions here, as at every stage in the Stockholm project, have convinced Stephen that he was right to choose the manufacturing industry as his career. He says that 'engineering means problem solving and it provides the opportunity to see exactly what you have achieved'. He feels part of the Eurostar success, just as he will one day get a special thrill from travelling by train from the airport to the centre of Stockholm.

Do pay and incentives motivate?

Traditional payment systems based on **time rates** (i.e. the number of hours worked) are necessary for many jobs – where output cannot be measured, where quality is so important the job should not be hurried, or where the speed of work cannot be controlled by the workers. With this system, workers cannot earn more if they work harder.

The **payment by results** method is often used for production workers whose output can be measured. Here, workers can earn more if they work harder.

Much research since Herzberg has confirmed the importance of firms creating the right conditions where workers can satisfy their higher needs and thus work harder. Important though this is, many companies today also encourage motivation by operating **incentive schemes** which involve a merit award being paid for extra performance.

Merit awards should, however, not be regularly paid, but awarded on appraisal. Otherwise they become expected as a right, not a reward. As Robert Townsend also points out, in *Up the Organisation*, 'Rewarding outstanding performances is important. Much more neglected is the equally important need to make sure that the underachievers don't get rewarded. This is more painful, so it doesn't get done very often.'

An extension of the incentive principle is **profit sharing**, where employees get a bonus according to the profit made by the company, sometimes linked to the issue of shares. The John Lewis Partnership introduced a profit-sharing scheme as long ago as 1929. Apart from the motivating aspects of such schemes, they do also have the advantage of encouraging workers to identify with the company.

Does participation in decision making motivate?

————

Much research has been done which shows that where workers participate in decision making, motivation is enhanced through them becoming more involved and committed and feeling that their opinions matter. On a more basic level, it is recognised that when workers' opinions influence a particular course of action being taken, they are far more determined to go all out to make that course of action work, rather than if it is just someone else's decision handed down for them to carry out.

Worker participation can take place on different levels. At one end of the scale are **consultative committees**, found in many companies. Worker representatives elected to these committees can influence decisions concerning a wide range of everyday issues affecting the company. At the other end of the scale, in some companies **worker representatives** are appointed to the board and have a chance to influence major policy decisions. However, critics of this system argue that workers are not capable of making any long-term policy decisions.

Some European firms have avoided this problem by adopting a dual system. This consists of a top-level board which is equivalent to the traditional board of directors and makes overall policy decisions, and a second-level board, including worker representatives, which is responsible for day-to-day management.

The role of trade unions today

————

Trade unions were founded in response to the harsh working conditions in the factories and mines of the early Industrial Revolution. Workers realised that they had more power standing together than on their own. Therefore they grouped together to act collectively, electing representatives to bargain on behalf of all the union members. Later, these local workplace initiatives joined together to form national unions.

There are now 260 unions in the UK with just over 8.5 million members, about one third of the workforce. Although trade unions were founded by manual workers, almost half of members today work in services such as banking or retailing. Nearly 40 per cent of union members are women, so the stereotype of a union member as a male manual worker is becoming less accurate.

There are four main types of union:

- **General unions**, which represent workers in a range of industries, such as the GMB (General Municipal and Boilermakers' Union).
- **Craft unions**, which represent workers from a group of industries who share a particular skill, such as the National Union of Lock and Metal Workers.
- **Industrial unions**, representing workers in a particular industry, whatever their skill, such as the NUM (National Union of Mineworkers).
- **White collar unions**, which represent clerical workers such as the NUJ (National Union of Journalists).

Trade unions negotiate with employers by means of **collective bargaining** to improve pay, working conditions and job security. At the local level, the elected **shop stewards** take up many individual grievances with management. The most common complaints are about health and safety and about legal issues such as contracts of employment plus threats of redundancy or dismissal. In recent years there has been a marked increase in the use of unions' legal services, as workers have sought some protection from a harsh economic climate. In the year to April 1994, trade unions won a record £335 million in legal compensation for members who suffered injury or ill health because of their work.

When disputes cannot be resolved between union and management, there are two avenues that can be explored. The **Advisory Conciliation and Arbitration Service (ACAS)** was set up in 1975 to offer help and ways of resolving disputes between unions and employers. Conciliation means bringing both sides together and encouraging them to settle their differences, while arbitration means hearing the case put by each side then deciding on the appropriate outcome. In individual cases, **industrial tribunals** enable workplace disputes to be settled legally.

The influence of the law over the position of workers and unions has made it important to attempt to influence the government in its legislative programme. Most of the larger unions belong to the **Trades Union Congress (TUC)**, which represents the union movement in discussions with the British government or the European Union. The **Confederation of British Industry (CBI)** performs the same role on behalf of most large businesses in the country. In the past, these organisations needed only to influence the British government. Now the laws established by the European Union can outrank those within Britain, so issues such as the right to strike may be taken out of the hands of the British Parliament.

WHAT DO PEOPLE THINK OF TRADE UNIONS?

Trade union membership has fallen by nearly 40 per cent from its peak in 1979. There have been four main reasons for this:

- The rise in unemployment.
- The changing patterns in employment, from manufacturing to services and from full- to part-time or temporary work.
- The reduction in the strength of unions due to changes in the law.
- The damage to the image of unions caused by highly publicised strikes during the 1970s and early 1980s.

Yet there is now evidence of a shift in public

attitudes. A 1993 Gallup survey found that 71 per cent of the adults polled considered unions 'a good thing'. The same survey found that 55 per cent believed the balance of power in industry had tilted too far in the direction of management compared with a mere 5 per cent who said the trade unions had the advantage. These positive findings were confirmed by the public support for the rail strikes of mid-1994.

Supporters of trade unions argue that they are essential for protecting the interests of employees who might otherwise get a raw deal from powerful employers. Yet critics believe that union wage claims can cause inflation and unemployment by pricing workers out of jobs. Another charge frequently levelled at unions is that they undermine the competitiveness of British industry because of opposition to technical progress and changing working practices. However, a survey by ACAS of 650 employers has shown that 'the presence of trade unions has not appeared to inhibit the introduction of new working practices'.

Among these new approaches have been the Japanese-inspired agreements between employers and unions involving single-union deals, multiskilled working and (sometimes) no-strike clauses. Originated by companies such as Toshiba UK in Plymouth and Nissan UK in Durham, these approaches involve a long-term commitment to workplace cooperation and investment. Their importance for attracting foreign investment to Britain cannot be overestimated.

In his 1994 book, *The Future of the Trade Unions*, Robert Taylor of the *Financial Times* concludes that it 'is a profound mistake' to believe that 'unions have become obsolete'. He sees them as 'allies of management in the negotiation of workplace change . . . where consensus is much more vital than competition in the achievement of corporate success'. In other words unions can succeed by working in partnership with employers.

ACTIVITY

Attitude battery towards the role of trade unions

On a copy of the table below, list the advantages and disadvantages of trade unions. Use the points mentioned in the text and any other points you can think of. You should have 10 statements in all.

	Statements	Agree strongly	Agree	Neither agree nor disagree	Disagree	Strongly disagree
Advantages						
Disadvantages						

Put a tick in the box which sums up your attitude towards each statement. What does your attitude battery reveal about your underlying attitudes to trade unions?

CASE STUDY

Mitsubishi Electric Europe (B.V.) – managing change

'Whatever Maslow or any other theorist says, I know that happy staff work better'. This statement by Neville Reyner, executive vice-president, Electronic Products Group of Mitsubishi Electric Europe, could be seen as unbusinesslike. Yet any director of a business that has grown tenfold in 10 years must be taken seriously. Especially when his own divisions of the business have an annual turnover of more than £120 million.

Mitsubishi Electric is less well known than its car-producing sister company, but it is a major force in consumer and industrial electronics. In Britain it produces televisions, videos, Apricot computers and air conditioning units. In total, the company employs over 2,000 people in Britain, with another 1,000 elsewhere in Europe (and some 900,000 worldwide).

The company's rapid growth since its 1978 origins in Britain threatened to make its sales and distribution centre less responsive and efficient. So the management response was to adopt a two-pronged approach:

● To work towards the international version of the BS 5750 quality assurance scheme (ISO 9002).
● To actively strive to stimulate workforce involvement by empowerment and the promotion of teamworking.

The move towards ISO 9002 was valuable in identifying weaknesses in the existing procedures within the business. For example, it emerged that if a customer sent a product back, up to six different people might be involved at the Mitsubishi depot. This maximised cost while minimising the chance of responding speedily to the customer's complaints or changed needs.

As inefficiencies emerged, it became clear that there would be consequences for Mitsubishi personnel. If just one person was responsible for a customer complaint instead of six, what would happen to those cut out of the new procedure? Mr Reyner's view is clear: that every effort should be made to avoid redundancies resulting from finding more efficient ways of working. 'Some companies can be too quick to cut staff. I believe in expanding our business so that new jobs emerge. Then we can retrain those whose own job is no longer needed.' Nevertheless, Mr Reyner is aware that problems may arise if employees do not want to be retrained.

Obtaining its ISO 9002 award took Mitsubishi over two years. Yet the focus of staff and management time upon quality yielded many spin-off benefits. It showed that involving the workforce in discussions and decisions about how the company operates could provide direct benefits from employee suggestions and indirect benefits from higher motivation. To capture the interest shown by staff in higher quality, the company built quality improvement teams (QIT) into its quality system.

Each product division of the business has a QIT consisting of representatives from engineering, marketing, sales and customer service. The team meets regularly to discuss any problems in meeting the standards set within the quality award. It can also look for ways of upgrading the quality targets set by Mitsubishi.

The process of empowerment proved easiest to establish in the electronics division that Mr Reyner set up in 1984. This was because the culture within this operation had always been democratic and based upon teamwork. The division introduced a system of customer focus teams ensuring regular meetings to agree how to provide total customer satisfaction. This process included regular meetings with large customers and came up with ideas such as using electronic data interchange (EDI) to establish a direct computer link to ensure faster, more efficient communication between Mitsubishi and its customers.

These customer focus teams have been so successful in providing total customer satisfaction in the UK that the idea has now been extended throughout Europe, Japan and the USA. Global customer focus teams are now being set up to ensure that improved relationships with customers are made on a multinational basis.

To what extent are Mitsubishi's approaches to personnel management the result of Japanese influence? On the face of it, a great deal, as Mitsubishi UK is headed by a Japanese and several of the senior executives are on five year secondments from Japan. In fact, much of the driving force has been from British managers, keen to keep abreast of modern management practices. Indeed, since the adoption of ISO 9002 in Britain, Mitsubishi divisions in Japan have decided to apply for this quality assurance certificate.

The main significance of Mitsubishi's Japanese parentage has been to ensure that long-term teambuilding approaches can be given the time needed to establish an upward flow of ideas and improvements. Hasty staff cutbacks during a tough year could undermine the whole approach to human relations within the company. Yet many British companies – even profitable ones – have done just that in recent years.

Mitsubishi Electric Europe has set itself the mission to 'become one of the leading corporate citizens of Europe, achieving sufficient profitability to ensure continuing success and investment'. So far they have achieved that balance between responsibility and success.

 DISCUSSION POINTS

1 *What advantages could a firm expect from involving staff in quality teams?*
2 *Why is it important that most Japanese firms offer staff a lifetime employment guarantee?*

From personnel to human resource management

Flexibility and change have become the most commonly used words in personnel vocabulary. In some ways this represents progress. Yesterday's nine to five career is rapidly disappearing, to be replaced by more part-time opportunities and fixed-term contracts. Ten years ago, all the economists working at BP's Head Office were salaried, permanent staff. Today most work on two- or three-year contracts, renewable if performance is good enough. This makes life less certain, but may prevent employees slipping into a dull routine.

These changes have coincided with the transformation of many personnel departments into human resource departments. HRM (human resource management) has two main features:

- The acceptance that staff attitudes and skills represent a vital element in a firm's success or failure, therefore the management of human resources should form part of the overall strategy/business plan.
- The desire to analyse and develop people's individual talents, instead of treating 'the workforce' as a homogenous group, with the same needs and rewards.

Few would argue with the first of these features. The acceptance of the key role of employees in company success has helped make training a higher priority and put pressure on the government to improve the quality of academic and vocational education in Britain.

The second aspect of human resource management has caused more controversy, however. Supporters speak highly of the greater emphasis HRM has given to:

- Psychological testing during recruitment.
- The use of appraisal schemes to measure employees' achievements and to set new goals for the coming year; often the result of the appraisal will affect the employee's income through performance related pay (for instance an appraisal rating as excellent might lead to a salary increase of 10 per cent).
- Individualised training programmes to help each employee develop the skills needed to achieve their goals.
- Questioning whether full-time, permanent staff are always necessary and bringing in part-time, temporary or sub-contracted staff where this is more economic or suitable.
- More careful analysis of those to be made redundant; in the past redundancies were usually made on the basis of 'last in first out', in other words the newest staff would be the first to go; today HRM professionals analyse attendance records, appraisal reports and even conduct psychological tests to select those to be made redundant.

Critics, however, see these aspects of HRM as potentially damaging to workplace morale and therefore performance. Appraisal schemes can lead to accusations of favouritism, with 'yes-men' getting salary increases denied to others who are more productive, but more critical of their boss. Morale might also be damaged by cutting the permanent workforce in favour of temporary, more flexible staffing. The work of both Maslow and Herzberg shows that job security is a necessary underpinning of employee motivation.

Despite these doubts about HRM, the approach can be defended on the grounds that British firms need to become more competitive. If that requires a more active approach to the management of people, it must still be preferable to company failures and therefore redundancy for all the staff. There remains the possibility, however, that research will cast doubt on whether practices such as appraisal do lead to greater efficiency, in which case the critics will be proved right.

ACTIVITY

Stylair Ltd: role-play exercise in resolving conflict

GENERAL BACKGROUND

Stylair Ltd is a medium-sized private company based in Birmingham. No longer a small family firm, it now employs 430 workers and manufactures a range of electric hairdryers. In the last decade, the company has grown rapidly, profits having increased by 35 per cent each year. This rapid growth has been achieved by Stylair's strategy of supplying well-designed products aimed at the middle range of the market. In recent years, they have experienced considerable competition from other UK manufacturers and have tried to combat this by developing export markets and by keeping costs down.

During its growth, Stylair has experienced no industrial relations problems, though recently some of the workforce have been expressing a few grievances.

BACKGROUND TO THE DISPUTE

Stylair's managing director, Louisa Whittaker, keeps a regular eye on the levels of overtime worked. In her last meeting with the production manager, Mike Hutchings, she mentioned her concern that the level of overtime worked by the maintenance team of six men had been rather high during the last six months. She queried why so much overtime had been done and asked Mike to check that overtime was not being abused.

The following morning, Mike called George Collins, the maintenance supervisor, into his office and told him that the company wanted to clamp down on unnecessary overtime. From now on, overtime would not be allowed without Mike's personal authorisation. George replied that the maintenance men would not like this, as they had come to depend on a certain amount of overtime in their take-home pay. Besides,

some machines could only be repaired outside normal working hours.

At lunch that day, George informed his men that management had decided that from now on overtime would no longer be worked. After a heated discussion in the works canteen, the men went back to work after lunch, still complaining angrily about the new ruling.

Ten days later, one of the machines broke down, in the midst of producing a large export order for an important new overseas customer. George allocated Mandy Johnson and Dave Hopkins to fix the machine urgently. At the end of the day Mike found out from George that Mandy and Dave had gone home at 5 p.m., leaving the machine half repaired, in spite of George having asked them to work on and finish it. When Mike insisted that he wanted the machine repaired straight away, otherwise the important export order would not be ready for shipment on the agreed date, George told him that Mandy and Dave were not prepared to work overtime because of the company's new 'overtime ban'.

At this point, Mike decided he ought to inform Louisa Whittaker of the problem. When Louisa heard what had happened, she asked to see everyone concerned, first thing the next morning, in her office.

THE BRIEF

In groups of five, you will be asked to act out the situation in Louisa Whittaker's office the next day. When you have decided which role you are going to play and have read all the following descriptions of the characters, you will need to act out your role, bringing out your side of the story, in relation to the other people involved. The group's eventual aim is to resolve the dispute.

ROLE DESCRIPTIONS

Louisa Whittaker, managing director

Age 54, married with two children. Bought the company 15 years ago, when it was struggling, with the redundancy money from her previous job as marketing manager with a well-known company. Highly respected by the workers, though they see less of her nowadays as the company has expanded.

Mike Hutchings, production manager

Age 39, unmarried. Loyal, works long hours and is ambitious. Aims to be a director of the firm one day and is keen to show he has a firm grip of things. Has worked his way up from the shop floor.

George Collins, maintenance supervisor

Age 56, married with three children. Has been with the firm since it started. Was a supervisor when Mike started as a trainee with the firm. A steady, reliable employee. Prefers the way things were done in the old days and is looking forward to his retirement.

Mandy Johnson, mechanic

Age 34, married. Been with the firm two and a half years. Good at her job but does not go looking for extra work. A bit of a loner, she never goes out with the others on Fridays for a drink after work. Can get 'in a huff' at times.

Dave Hopkins, mechanic

Age 28, married with two young children. Has been with the firm 12 years, since he joined as an apprentice at 16. He likes it there and is a good worker. Enjoys going out with the others on Friday nights and gets on well with everyone.

 # DISCUSSION POINTS

1 Why might Louisa Whittaker have been concerned about overtime levels?

2 How far can the dispute be said to have arisen through poor communications in the organisation:

   a) downwards from the management to the shop floor?

   b) upwards from the shop floor to the management?

3 Why is there a need for different communication channels in the firm now, compared to when it was a small firm?

4 To what extent might the situation have been aggravated by possible personality clashes between the people involved?

5 Taking each person in turn, describe how far you think he was responsible for the dispute which arose.

6 How was the dispute eventually resolved in each of your groups?

7 What might have happened if the dispute had not ended at this stage?

8 How might the presence of a trade union have:

   a) helped

   b) hindered

   the resolution of this dispute?

9 In what ways is this situation:

   a) typical

   b) untypical

   of the way disputes can happen?

Finance

IN ASSOCIATION WITH

PRICEWATERHOUSECOOPERS 🅟

When running a business there are two main financial priorities: generating enough cash to pay the bills, and enough profit to satisfy the shareholders and to finance growth. So, are cash and profit not the same thing? Surprisingly, they are not. To help explain the difference, cash flow will be analysed in detail, followed by profit.

Cash flow

Cash flow is the difference between the flows of cash into and out of a business over a period of time. For example, if a firm starts up by spending £40,000 of cash on premises and materials in its first month, but receives only £500 from customers, its month 1 cash flow is minus £39,500.

Cash flow can be looked at in two ways:

- As a way of predicting the future state of a firm's bank balance (a cash-flow forecast).
- As a record of how a firm has obtained and used cash over the recent past (a cash-flow statement).

This chapter will look at cash-flow forecasting only. This is especially important when starting a new

business, as few firms start with capital to spare. If a sales forecast proves too optimistic (and this is a common problem) or if production proves slower than expected, the firm may struggle to keep paying its bills. For an example of the key role of cash-flow forecasting, take the case of Clare Kilby:

Clare decided, fresh from catering college, to use £4,000 of savings to start a high quality, premium-priced catering service. 'Crystal Cuisine' would offer to plan, cook, deliver and serve superb and beautifully presented food to important business meetings or exclusive dinner parties. This would require a large, well-equipped kitchen, a van and a high initial outlay on publicity. Having completed the cash-flow forecast shown opposite, Clare was able to persuade a friend to come in as a partner (investing £2,000) and a bank to lend £5,000 for a good, second-hand van.

A cash-flow forecast shows two key things about money: *when* and *how much*, in the case of both incoming and outgoing funds. For example, Clare found a kitchen available for hire at £1,200 per month. She planned to move in at the start of January and expected to need £600 of extra kitchen equipment. As she only intended to start advertising in February, cash inflows would start in that month.

Crystal Cuisine – Year 1 cash-flow forecast				
(all figures in £s)				
	January	February	March	April	May–Dec
Start-up capital	11,000				
CASH INFLOW	–	500	4,000	5,000	52,000
CASH OUTFLOW					
Start-up costs	600	7,300	–		
Running costs	1,200	1,400	2,600	3,100	26,000
Wages	400	600	1,000	1,200	13,000
NET CASH FLOW	(2,200)	(8,800)	400	700	13,000
CUMULATIVE CASH	+8,800	0	+400	+1,100	+14,100

Crystal Cuisine – Year 1 cash-flow forecast

This forecast convinced Clare's bank to grant her an overdraft facility of up to £1,000, in case February's zero balance slipped into the red. She was able to start up her business and – after a month or two of struggle – it has become a great success.

Even when a business is up and running, forecasting cash-flows is important. Most firms have periods in the year when cash is especially tight. For example, bookshops often make a quarter of their year's sales in just one month – December. So, in the autumn they have to plough a lot of cash into buying stock to build up the stock of books that will be sold for Christmas.

If a firm entered a period of **negative cash flow** without having forecast it or discussed the situation with their bankers, one of two things would probably happen. One is that the firm may be unable to pay bills to suppliers of raw materials, packaging, electricity or even labour costs (i.e. unable to pay staff their wages). This situation would be hard to

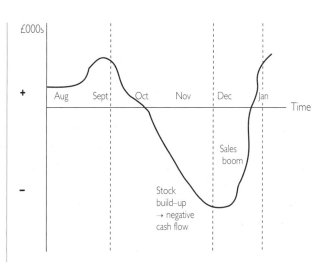

Cash-flow graph for a bookshop

sustain for long. The other possibility is that the firm may write out cheques to pay the bills, either going into an unauthorised overdraft (which banks charge very heavily for) or finding that the bank refuses to honour them (so the cheques 'bounce').

By making a cash-flow forecast, a firm is able to adjust its actions to avoid calamity or to maximise potential benefits. For example, if it expects to go severely into the red during the autumn, it could take various actions to prevent this happening, such as:

- Negotiating with suppliers to delay cash payments until the new year.
- Postponing cash outgoings, such as replacing company vans or equipment, until the new year.
- Working much harder at the careful organisation required to delay the ordering and arrival of stock so that it arrives just in time to meet customer demand.

On the other hand, perhaps the cash-flow forecast shows a four-month period of really high cash balances, such as in a bookshop during and after Christmas. If a firm is confident that it will have plenty of surplus cash for a few months, it can open an interest-paying deposit account or use the cash to make a short-term investment. Either approach may provide a useful boost to a firm's profit.

Profit and loss

Cash flow is straightforward enough to understand, but why is profit any different? There are many answers to this problem, some of which are given in Table 7.1. So, a firm that has recently declared a £60,000 profit may, in fact, be desperate for cash because its customers are stalling payment or because a large loan is due to be repaid.

Actual results equate to cash-flow: cash in = goals scored; cash outflow = goals against. It is easy to know who won and who lost. The calculation of profit is like Fantasy League™ schemes, however, where you have to make assumptions about what it is worth to have made the pass to the person who scores. You might even deduct a point because a booking could lead to a suspension later on (in accounting, this would be known as a provision). In other words, calculating profit involves taking a wider view of the situation and taking into account many other factors.

This book does not need or want to go into full details about the calculation of profit. However it will be useful to provide some indication of the ways in which the calculation of profit is different from the calculation of cash flows. Table 7.1 shows how different, everyday financial events are recorded in a firm's accounts.

TABLE 7.1

Financial event	Cash flow	Profit	Notes to profit calculation
Sale to a customer	When cash arrives	When product is delivered	Cash may arrive months later
£40,000 invested by new shareholders	When cash arrives	Not recorded	The £40,000 is extra capital, not profit made by the firm
£20,000 of supplies bought on credit	No record (until later, when cash is paid)	When supplies are delivered	Cash is paid later, but profit records the transaction straight away
A £50,000 bank loan is repaid	When cash leaves	Not recorded	£50,000 less capital, but no loss has been made on the firm's trading

The important message here is that profit is not the same as cash. To be successful in business, it is vital to realise that a manager needs to forecast both its cash flows and its profit. The latter can be forecast or recorded through the profit and loss account.

A profit and loss account (often known as the P & L) shows the various deductions that are made from a firm's revenue, ending up with the figure that is left for reinvestment in the business. This, the 'bottom line', is crucial as it shows how much the firm is making to help it grow in the future. Without reinvested profit a firm will stand still or decline.

Below is a simplified version of the 1995 accounts for Denby Pottery:

Denby Group plc Accounts for year end October 30th

	1995 (£000s)	1994 (£000s)
Sales turnover	**25,795**	**21,915**
Cost of sales	13,314	11,125
Overheads	7,540	6,240
Interest charges	179	420
Pre-tax profit	**4,762**	**4,130**
Taxation	1,571	1,364
Dividends	1,153	924
Retained profit	**2,038**	**1,842**

Raising finance

In order to start a business, capital must be raised. Start-up capital usually comes mainly from the founders of the business or their family, for unless the founders are willing to put their own funds at risk, who else would be silly enough to do so? In addition, whereas interest on bank loans has to be paid even when times are bad, owners' capital does not receive a fixed rate of return. This enhances flexibility in the early years of trading.

At this initial stage, entrepreneurs willing to put in their own capital could also turn to several possible sources of extra investment funds. The first destination is likely to be a visit to their bank manager. The bank will not invest share capital into a new firm, but may be willing to provide loans to supplement the start-up funds. This loan capital will only be provided, though, if the firm demonstrates the ability to repay it – with a plausible cash-flow forecast, accompanied by a profit and loss account. Security such as property may be needed to back up the loan, but is not as important as evidence that the loan can be repaid.

If the bank is worried about the security of its loans, but still believes the business has a good chance of succeeding, it could offer to lend via the government's Loan Guarantee Scheme. This scheme guarantees the bank that if the business fails, the government will repay from 70 to 85 per cent of what is owed. This limits the bank's risk and so makes it more willing to provide the loan. The only downside to the Loan Guarantee Scheme is that the borrower has to pay between 0.5 and 1.5 per cent extra every year to the government.

What if someone has a great business idea – perhaps an invention – but has too little capital to make the bank even consider lending? There are still some possibilities. One is to convince a Venture Capital provider that your idea and your own track record make you worth backing. This will not be easy, because although Venture Capital houses accept a relatively high level of risk, they pride themselves upon the care they take over each application. As their careful checks are expensive to carry out, Venture Capital houses are rarely interested in investments of below £200,000. Also, they insist upon a share stake in the business (perhaps 30 per cent of the shares) so that they can share in the high profits made by the occasional Body Shop.

Once a firm is up and running, statistics show that reinvested profit is by far the biggest source of extra capital to finance growth. In addition to reinvested profit, there are many other ways in which a firm can find short-, medium- or long-term finance (see Tables 7.2, 7.3 and 7.4).

Short-term finance can be used to:

● Bridge temporary finance gaps when customers pay late or a sudden, rush order requires a large sum to buy raw materials.
● Get through periods when cash-flow is poor for seasonal reasons.
● Cover temporary needs for extra funds due to unexpected problems or opportunities.

Medium-term finance can be used to:

● Finance the purchase of assets with a two to five year life, such as vehicles and computers.
● Replace an overdraft which is difficult to clear and is proving expensive.
● Finance a change in strategy, such as to switch marketing focus from Britain to the whole of Europe.

TABLE 7.2 *Types of short-term finance*

Source of finance	Advantages	Disadvantages
Bank overdraft	Simple to arrange. Flexible, as amounts borrowed can vary up to the limit arranged. Relatively cheap in the short term, as interest is charged only on the actual amount borrowed, for the number of days overdrawn.	Interest charged is between 2.5 per cent and 4 per cent over bank base lending rate, so can work out expensive over long periods. If limit is exceeded the overdraft facility can be withdrawn and immediate repayment demanded.
Trade credit	Improves the flow of money as suppliers often give as long as three months to pay invoices. A free form of credit.	The prompt payment discount which many firms offer is lost if the trade credit is used. If payment is made after the credit period, suppliers may refuse to send goods in future, or may insist on cash in advance.
Debt factoring	Capital tied up in money owed by customers is released. The factoring company takes over the debt and advances up to 80 per cent of the amount owed straight away. This improves the firm's cash flow. The factoring company then sends out invoices and chases up the debtor, paying the remainder of the debt to the firm when the customer settles up – less their charge.	Factoring companies can charge as much as 5 per cent of the bill for their service. They tend only to be interested in handling bills from firms with sales of over £1 million a year.

Long-term finance can be used to:

● Provide start-up capital to finance the business for its whole life span.
● Finance the purchase of assets with a longer life, such as buildings.
● Provide expansion capital for large projects, such as building a new factory or taking over another business.

TABLE 7.3 *Types of medium-term finance (two to five years)*

Source of finance	Advantages	Disadvantages
Bank term loan	Financial planning is made easier as repayments are made in regular instalments and the interest rate is often fixed.	Small businesses generally pay higher rates as they are seen as presenting a higher risk.
Leasing	When vehicles and equipment are leased or rented from a leasing company, the firm is able to use equipment which it could not otherwise afford to buy outright. Working capital can then be used for other purposes. Leased equipment can be changed when it becomes obsolete, unlike purchased equipment which has to be kept for longer to recover the initial investment.	The vehicles and equipment which are leased are not owned by the firm. The rental charges add up over a period of time, to the point where the firm has effectively more than paid for the goods even though the goods cannot be classed as company assets, because they are still owned by the company renting them out.
Hire purchase	After an initial down-payment for the vehicle or equipment, goods are purchased in instalments over a period of 2 years. This means the cost is spread and is more manageable than an up-front payment for outright purchase. Unlike leased goods those bought on hire purchase are owned after the last repayment is made.	Goods remain the property of the finance house until full repayment has been made, so if any payments are missed the finance house can repossess the goods. A more expensive form of borrowing than bank loans.

ACTIVITY

Choosing the most appropriate source of finance

For each of the following descriptions, state which source of finance you think it is most appropriate to use. Explain your decision in each case.

1. A firm that wishes to finance a major purchase of land for a new factory.

2. A successful firm where the owners are willing to dilute financial control in order to expand, by giving up part of their equity.

3. A firm that has borrowed as much as it can but cannot pay its expenses until slow-paying customers pay their bills.

4. A firm that has to decide between paying a bill from

TABLE 7.4 *Types of long-term finance (over 5 years)*

Source of finance	Advantages	Disadvantages
Owners' savings (in the case of a sole trader or partnership)	Owners use their own capital (from a second mortgage, life insurance policy, savings etc.) to inject capital into the business, which reduces the amount borrowed on which interest has to be paid. Owners retain more control than if financial control is diluted by the sale of shares.	Owners' capital is tied up and cannot easily be taken out of business. Owners' capital is at risk if business fails – they are liable to lose their own home and other possessions.
Sale of shares (in the case of a private limited company or public limited company)	The main advantage of issuing shares is that the shareholders have **limited liability** if the business fails. Personal possessions are not at risk and their liability is limited to the actual capital invested. Capital is raised by issuing shares (which are a proportion of what the company is worth) to investors, who are encouraged to buy by the promise of receiving **dividends** or capital gain on their shares, due to an increase in the share price. Shares can be sold as **preference shares** which offer a fixed return and have priority when dividends are paid over ordinary shareholders. **Ordinary shares** offer a variable return as profits change from year to year, according to how well the company has done.	The administrative cost of issuing shares is high. It is difficult to estimate the market price of shares, though this problem can be avoided if they are issued by **tender**, where investors state how much they are willing to pay for them. The price of shares can go up or down and shareholders may have to sell at a lower price than they bought at. A listing or **quotation** on the Stock Exchange is needed for PLCs, so a company's shares can be bought or sold on the exchange. This is difficult to obtain as financial requirements are stringent in order to safeguard the interests of people buying and selling shares.
Reinvested profits	Capital can be raised by the company reinvesting or ploughing back the profits made at the end of the year, after expenses and dividends to shareholders have been paid.	Profits may be scarce or non-existent, especially in times of recession. Expansion may be slow and limited for companies relying on self-financed growth.
Mortgage loans	Capital is often supplied by pension or insurance funds for a loan over 25–30 years for buildings or land, with the asset as security.	The loans are usually only given when large sums are required.
Venture capital loans	Capital is supplied by venture capital firms who accept a certain degree of risk as being inevitable. Most venture capitalists also provide help in the form of back-up management and financial expertise. The government's **Enterprise Investment Scheme** offers incentives to private investors willing to invest in unquoted companies.	Most venture capitalists are only interested in loans for more than £50,000 and some only consider ventures where more than £250,000 is involved, as the administration costs are not worthwhile on smaller projects. They charge a negotiation fee for arranging the finance. They generally expect a non-controlling **equity stake** of 20–40 per cent in the firm's capital, as a return for their investment.
Government loans	Capital can be raised for eligible companies from local authorities, government enterprise agencies and regional selective assistance. Capital can also be raised from the EU.	The vetting procedures needed to minimise risk can cause long delays in obtaining the grants.
Debenture loans	Individuals can supply capital to a company in the form of long-term loans called **debentures** which have to be repaid on an agreed date. These repayments take priority over payments to all other shareholders.	Generally the company has to offer some security for the loan, which can be sold if the company cannot meet the repayments. In the case of a fixed debenture this is a specific asset such as a building, and in the case of a floating debenture it can be any asset owned by the company.

British Telecom or a bill from a supplier, both of which were received two weeks ago.

5 An established firm, quoted on the Stock Exchange, which wishes to raise money from the public to be repaid after a specific period of time.

6 A firm that wishes to spread the cost of high capital outlay on equipment and has borrowed the maximum possible from the bank.

7 A firm which will create many new jobs and is being set up in a depressed area.

8 A successful, well-run, private limited company which has expanded as far as possible on self-financed growth.

9 A firm that has bills from suppliers which are due for payment now, though money owed by customers will not come in for a few weeks.

10 A small firm started by an entrepreneur who intends to trade on a small scale initially and who wishes to retain full control of the business.

11 A firm whose owners intend to expand at a steady rate without diluting financial control and without borrowing too much.

12 A firm in a high-technology industry which does not wish to purchase all the expensive equipment it needs.

13 A firm that wishes to raise finance to invest in buildings and equipment.

CASE STUDY

PricewaterhouseCoopers' Private Finance Initiative in Hereford and Worcester

INTRODUCTION

PricewaterhouseCoopers was created in 1998 by the merger of two firms – Price Waterhouse and Coopers & Lybrand – each with historical roots going back some 150 years and originating in London. PricewaterhouseCoopers, the world's largest professional services organisation, helps its clients build value, manage risk and improve their performance. Drawing on the talents of more than 140,000 people in 152 countries, it provides a full range of business advisory services to leading global, national and local companies and to public institutions. These services include audit, accounting and tax advice, management, information technology and human resource consulting; financial advisory services including mergers & acquisitions, business recovery, project finance and litigation support; business process outsourcing services; and legal services through a global network of affiliated law firms. The new, combined organisation is the result of the continuing growth in the international economy.

At PricewaterhouseCoopers, there are six services lines or departments which cover different areas of specialisation. These are as follows:

- Assurance & Business Advisory Services
- Management Consulting Services
- Tax & Legal Services
- Financial Advisory Services
- Global Human Resource Solutions
- Business Process Outsourcing

In this case study the role of **Financial Advisory Services (FAS)** is explored with a focus on private finance initiatives. Their FAS team offers financial, economic and strategic advice to household names around the world. The five departments within FAS are:

- Business Recovery Services
- Dispute Analysis & Investigations
- Mergers & Acquisitions
- Project Finance & Privatisation
- Valuations & Shareholder Value

Project Finance & Privatisation
Governments (the public sector) and the private sector (companies) are increasingly working together. PricewaterhouseCoopers is experienced in advising both private and public sectors.

Private Finance Initiative (PFI)
The Conservative Government launched the Private Finance Initiative (PFI) in 1992 in a bid to deliver high quality and cost-effective public services whilst

avoiding the need to raise taxes in the short-term. PFI allows the public sector service providers to obtain or 'procure' those services, while placing the risks of buying and maintaining the asset with the private sector. In a PFI the Government body sets up a contract with a private company. The private company buys, builds and services the asset. The Government has use of the fully serviced asset for the period of the contract and at the end of this period, the Government will own the asset. The Government uses the fully serviced asset in exchange for a rental payment. Typical examples of PFI are projects requiring large investment such as schools, hospitals, road and rail links, waste disposal services and prison services.

PFIs are also utilised in building new schools. In the case of Falkirk, Scotland, a 25 year contract was signed between Falkirk Council and a company called Class 98 to provide three new secondary schools, a major secondary school extension and a special needs school at a cost of £70 million. This was the first PFI project involving the provision of a number of schools to be undertaken. The risks for the private sector in undertaking a PFI are many and it is the role of the negotiating team to assess how great are these risks and whether they would affect the completion of the project.

PFIs are also utilised in waste management services as in the following example in Hereford and Worcester. A number of different companies were involved in the disposal of waste in Hereford and Worcester, and in 1998, a number of their contracts were up for renewal. The local authorities decided to review the management of the waste services and ensure that this public service was cost-effective and complied with environmental targets.

The arrangements for disposal of the waste were almost exclusively through landfill, with a very low percentage of the waste committed to recycling or other forms of recovery (5–6%) and no incentives to improve on these levels. In a bid to reduce the level of landfill, the Labour Government substantially increased taxes levied on this form of waste disposal. This cost incentive, along with the requirement to meet environment targets and the benefits of an integrated contract, encouraged Hereford & Worcester local

authorities to review PFI as a new means of procuring their waste disposal services.

The local authorities were also keen to take advantage of 'PFI credits' which provided local authorities with a financial incentive to identify opportunities for a PFI. In this instance PricewaterhouseCoopers were brought in on behalf of the local authority to provide financial advice and assistance in managing the procurement process. The Hereford & Worcester waste management project is the first fully-integrated waste management PFI. Set out below is a summary of the key issues involved in the development of this project.

1 **What is waste management?** Waste management consists of:
   ● Refuse collection from homes and industry
   ● Transportation of waste to the disposal sites
   ● Waste treatment and disposal
   ● Recycling and energy recovery
   ● Landfill management
2 **Environmental concerns.** The global drive to improve the management of waste and increase the amount of recycling has generated new global targets. The following apply in the UK:
   ● >25% waste recycled by 2000
   ● >40% waste recovered by 2005
   ● <60% waste buried in landfill sites by 2005
   Landfill sites are the primary means of disposing of waste in the UK. However, there is less land available and the effects of landfill on the environment remain unclear. In addition, the amount of waste is increasing as the number of households grows. There is increased use of 'waste to energy' incinerator plants which burn certain types of waste and require capital investment and planning permission, but these may be redundant in 25 years time. Uncertainty exists also over the effect of incineration on the environment.
3 **PFI – The right path?** A PFI in waste management allowed Hereford and Worcester local authorities the opportunity to integrate the various waste management systems into one contract, and gain access to capital investment and PFI government credits. The cost of the services was negotiated according to the level of services gained (amount of waste disposed) and included environmental targets for recycling with financial incentives if these were achieved. The concern was that this PFI tied the

authority into a long-term contract of 25 years during which time environmental laws may change.

4 The Contract and the Risks. The contract was agreed for 25 years with key recycling and recovery targets set with a minimum number of household waste tips and treatment facilities (landfill, 'waste to energy' plants, recycling stations) agreed. Risks are assessed and agreed for every PFI and these risks were identified and retained or transferred to the private sector.

5 Procurement process. The procurement process can be lengthy. More than two years elapsed between placing the advertisement in the recognised European trade journal, OJEC, and completing the negotiation process when FOCSA Services Ltd was selected as the 'preferred partner'.

6 Mechanism of payment. The arrangements for payment by Hereford and Worcester local authorities were included in the contract. These payments were based on the tonnage of waste processed with a supplement for recycling and recovery.

7 Concerns. Additional concerns to the local authorities include the threat of protestor action and whether a PFI provides a cost-effective solution.

Key Learning Points

The key learning points in this PFI were:

1 Clearly define the risk allocation and risks profile before selecting the preferred bidder.

2 Understand the risks a council will underwrite.

3 Be realistic in risk allocation.

4 Allocate resources necessary to complete the project.

5 Use experienced advisers.

Conclusion

The completion of the PFI means that Hereford and Worcester were the first local authorities to negotiate a PFI for a fully integrated waste management service. The contract is now in place to run for 25 years. The Financial Advisory Services at PricewaterhouseCoopers advised the local authority and managed the procurement process for the PFI.

This case study was originally written for the fourth edition of The Times 100 Case Studies with Business News, produced by MBA Publishing and Times Newspapers Ltd. For further information about Times 100 telephone 01937-541541.

ACTIVITY

1 What is a PFI? Explain why they were introduced.

2 Using a simple example, describe how a PFI works. In what way is a PFI similar to paying a mortgage?

3 Working in small groups, list 4 potential projects for your local community for PFI investment. For each project describe how local people would benefit.

4 Explain the meaning of the following words and phrases:
- public sector
- European procurement legislation
- capital
- long-term
- integrated solution
- interest rates
- negotiation
- recycling

5 Look at the Hereford & Worcester case study. Who benefited from this PFI? Explain how this provided a cost-effective solution for a local authority.

Break-even analysis

When considering whether to start up a business, nothing could be more important than an idea of how large a profit or how big a loss you might make. This can be shown by use of a break-even chart.

A **break-even chart** shows revenues and costs at all possible levels of output. From this, it is easy to see the *profit* at any level of output, as the profit is the difference between revenue and cost.

To construct a break-even chart, it is necessary to break costs down into two parts: fixed and variable. **Fixed costs** are those that do not vary as output varies, such as rent, salaries and interest charges. In other words, even in a month when sales are awful, these costs are as high as ever. **Variable costs**, by contrast, do vary in relation to output. In other words, if output slumps by 50 per cent, these costs may slump by the same proportion. Examples include raw material purchases, components and packaging costs.

CONSTRUCTING A BREAK-EVEN CHART

A break-even chart is a line graph showing total revenue and costs at all possible levels of output/demand, i.e. at every point from an output of nil through to the maximum the firm can produce. This enables the reader to see at a glance the profit at any output level that interests them (by looking at the vertical difference between revenue and costs).

For example: A firm selling 40,000 widgets per year has fixed costs of £50,000, variable costs of £1 per unit and a factory capable of producing 60,000 units. The widgets are priced at £3 each.

Quantity	Revenue (£)	Variable costs (£)	Fixed costs (£)	Total cost (£)
0	0	0	50,000	50,000
30,000	90,000	30,000	50,000	80,000
60,000	180,000	60,000	50,000	110,000

From this information a break-even chart can be drawn as follows, with £s on the vertical axis and output on the horizontal.

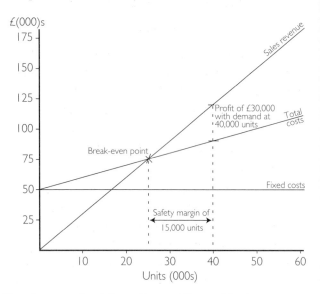

Break-even chart for a firm selling widgets

The chart can be used to show various things:

1 The break-even point. This is usually indicated by a vertical line down to cut the horizontal axis, i.e. to indicate the output level at which all costs are covered; beyond this output level the firm starts to make profits. In this case the break-even point is 25,000 units.

2 The safety margin. This is the amount by which demand and therefore output can fall before the firm starts making losses. As sales are currently 40,000 units, the firm can afford demand to fall by 15,000 units before output goes below the break-even point.

3 Profit or loss at a particular level of output. Here, the company's profit is the difference between revenue and costs at 40,000 units. As marked on the graph, this comes to £30,000.

ACTIVITY

Quik Kalc Ltd: analysing break-even points

You work in the financial department of Quik Kalc Ltd, a rapidly expanding firm which manufactures calculators, aimed at the 'volume' end of the market. Mr Singh, the senior accountant, has asked you to work out the exact level of output at which the firm breaks even or just recovers its

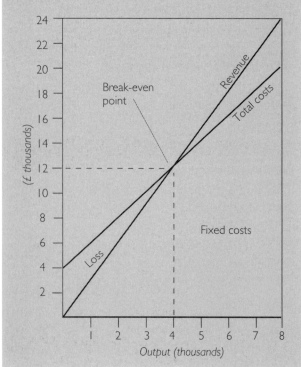

costs. Quik Kalc's fixed costs are £4,000. Each calculator costs £2 to make in terms of variable costs (labour and materials) and sells for £3. In order to work out the **break-even point**, you will need to use these figures when you fill in your copy of the table below to show the costs and revenue at different output levels.

Output (£)	Fixed costs (£)	Variable costs (£) (Multiply by output level)	Total costs (£) (Add fixed and variable costs)	Revenue (Multiply price by output)
0	4,000	0	4,000	0
1,000	4,000	2,000	6,000	3,000
2,000				
3,000				
4,000				
5,000				
6,000				
7,000				
8,000				

The results from the table you have filled in have been plotted on the previous page. You will see that the break-even point occurs when Quik Kalc produces 4,000 calculators. This can also be worked out by a simple calculation. One of their calculators costs £2 to make in terms of variable costs and sells for £3, so each calculator sold makes a contribution of £1 towards fixed costs. As the fixed costs are £4,000, this means 4,000 calculators have to be sold before the break-even point is reached. If Quik Kalc sells any more than 4,000 it makes a profit and if it sells any fewer it makes a loss. The greater the output, the greater the profit, though eventually a stage will be reached when the fixed costs will have to rise to cater for the increased production.

ACTIVITY

Analysing the factors affecting break-even points

Use the simple calculation method described above to work out the new break-even point (if any) in the following situations. (Figures remain the same unless otherwise stated.)

1 Quik Kalc begins to experience fierce competition and has to reduce the selling price of each calculator to £2.50.

2 Demand increases in the months before Christmas and Quik Kalc raises the selling price to £4 per calculator.

3 A shortage of raw materials encourages suppliers to put up their prices by £1 so the variable costs are now £3 per calculator.

4 A severe recession forces Quik Kalc to reduce the selling price to £2.

5 Explain why the break-even point changed in questions 1 and 2.

6 Why was it not possible to break even in questions 3 and 4?

Working capital

Once a business is up and running, a key aspect of good financial management is to keep a tight control of **working capital**. Working capital is the finance available for the day-to-day running of the business. It is sometimes known as circulating capital, because of the way it flows around the business (see the diagram on page 96).

Although this cycle appears neat and tidy, it can quite easily get out of control, especially if a sales boom is keeping the directors of a small firm so busy that they cannot make time to monitor the working capital. For instance, customers may not pay unless they are chased. This may mean that the firm has too little cash to pay for raw materials, leaving the factory idle and customers frustrated.

The key to good management of working capital is to have efficient systems. For instance, if stock levels are computer-monitored using laser scanning, the firm should know exactly what it holds in its stores. This ensures that extra materials will only be ordered when they are really needed, rather than just in case they are needed.

In addition to careful stock control, at least one employee should be responsible for credit control. This entails checking the creditworthiness of customers and then ensuring that they pay on time. If the firm lacks the market power to press customers to pay, the job of obtaining payment may be done better by a debt factor. This is a business which charges a fee for organising the collection of the sums owed by customers (see Table 7.2).

Another key component to controlling working capital is to set budgets that are monitored closely. **Budgets** are usually agreed before the start of a financial year, and represent the maximum a manager can spend on an item. For example, a brand manager may be given a budget of £620,000 for a year's advertising and promotions. The manager will have to decide how to split the money up between the months of the year; then the accounts department will send a statement each month showing how much has actually been spent compared with the budgeted level. This comparison is known as **the variance**.

By ensuring that managers know each month whether they are under- or over-spending, the budget and variance statement makes it quite easy for staff to cut back to avoid over-spending. Variance figures can also

highlight where and why an under- or over-spend has occurred. A typical example is shown in Table 7.5 below. Note that the variance column is calculated in relation to profit. Therefore revenue which is *lower* than forecast is a negative variance (in brackets), as are fixed costs which are *higher* than forecast.

TABLE 7.5 *A budget and variance statement*

	January			February		
	Budget	Actual	Variance	Budget	Actual	Variance
Revenue	85	80	(5)	95	86	(9)
Materials	36	34	2	42	39	3
Fixed costs	42	44	(2)	45	45	–
Profit	7	2	(5)	8	2	(6)
Year to date (Profit)	7	2	(5)	15	4	(11)

Note: All figures in £000s.

The figures in Table 7.5 show that although the firm's profit is much lower than forecast, the fault does not seem to lie with costs. The main cause of the profit shortfall is the lower than expected sales revenue. Having established this, the firm can decide whether the cause was outside the firm's control (such as a recession seizing the economy) or whether the business itself has made some poor decisions.

Conclusion

Financing and running a business – even if small – requires a great deal of knowledge and attention. If the planning is careful and the monitoring is constant, few firms get into financial trouble.

Yet even the best plans will go wrong sometimes, such as when a sudden consumer scare halts the purchase of a company's products. An unexpected collapse in revenue would wreck the calm planning of most companies. In this situation, as in many others, a close relationship with the company's bank manager can be useful. Together, a new strategy can be worked out.

Management

IN ASSOCIATION WITH

Dixons

Introduction: doing the right things

A good definition of a manager is 'An individual who is accountable for more work than he/she can do themselves and who gets some of it done through other people' (W Brown and E Jacques). This definition includes managers who function at all levels, from operational manager right up to the chief executive at the top of the organisation. The **span of control**, however, or number of employees whose work is directed by managers at different levels, will obviously vary.

Successful managers have invariably learnt the difference between efficiency and effectiveness. Managers who have the ability to 'do things right' will merely be efficient, but to be really effective a manager must 'do the right things' – in other words, produce results. Peter Drucker, in his book, *The Effective Executive*, describes five practices which are necessary for effectiveness.

Effective executives:

● **Know where their time goes.** 'They systematically manage the small amount of their time that they can control.'

● **Focus on outward contribution.** 'They start with the question "What results are expected of me?", rather than starting with what work needs to be done.'

● **Build on strengths.** This includes building on 'their own strengths, the strengths of their superiors, colleagues and subordinates and on the strengths in the situation – that is, on what they *can* do.'

● **Concentrate on a few major areas.** 'They force themselves to set priorities.'

● **Make effective decisions.** 'They make judgements after taking into account a variety of opposing viewpoints. The decisions they make are few but fundamental.'

What does a manager do?

The earliest attempt at isolating what a manager's job involves was made by Henri Fayol, whose writings were first published in English in 1947. Based on his own management experience in the French mining industry, he arrived at a definition of the role of a manager – which was to:

● **Forecast and plan** – examine the future and draw up a plan of action.
● **Organise** – build up the organisation's structure so that plans can be carried out effectively.
● **Command** – obtain the best possible performance from personnel.
● **Coordinate** – make sure each department's efforts harmonise with other departments.
● **Control** – make sure everything works according to plan.

Later on, in 1973, Henry Mintzberg's approach was more concerned with what managers *actually* do, as opposed to what they ought to do. On the basis of studies of managers' work activity, he showed in *The Nature of Managerial Work* that managers perform a wide variety of roles.

These 10 roles can be grouped into three broad areas:

● **Interpersonal** – the relationships a manager has to have with others.
● **Informational** – the collecting and passing on of information.
● **Decisional** – the making of different kinds of decisions.

Of course, Mintzberg recognised that these roles can be combined in a number of different ways according to the manager's own personality, the situation he or she is in, the kind of job he or she does and the general environment.

ACTIVITY

Classification of a manager's roles

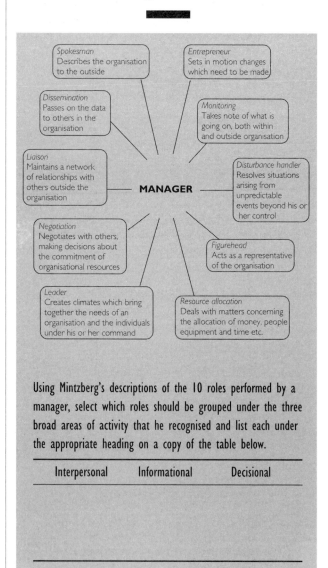

Using Mintzberg's descriptions of the 10 roles performed by a manager, select which roles should be grouped under the three broad areas of activity that he recognised and list each under the appropriate heading on a copy of the table below.

Interpersonal	Informational	Decisional

DISCUSSION POINTS

1 How many of the roles does your headteacher probably carry out?

2 Are some roles more important than others?

What qualities do managers need?

In 1988, a report called 'What Makes a Manager?' was published by the Institute of Manpower Studies (IMS), which looked at how 40 leading UK employers defined managerial skills. The report, reviewed by Michael Syrett in *Director* magazine, found that the qualities these employers looked for most often were the ability to communicate, leadership, judgement, initiative, organisational skills and motivation. Other attributes less frequently mentioned by employers, but still regarded as important, were planning, innovation, good appearance, interpersonal skills, maturity and numeracy.

One of the co-authors of the report, Wendy Hirsh, says that, 'The need for managers to deal with change was apparent in the frequent mention of adaptability, the capacity to deal with stress and the need for personal energy.' She added that, 'Employers also tend to look for "macho" managers with rather assertive personalities. Where sensitivity is needed, it tends to be expressed in terms of skills, for example the ability to work in teams, rather than in personality.'

In the next activity, you will be asked within groups of five to rank these management qualities yourselves and decide which *you* think are most important.

ACTIVITY

Ranking of management attributes

On your individual copy of the table below, rank each management attribute in order of importance from 1 to 16 and write the ranking in column 1. Rank the attribute you rate as being most important as 1, through to the least important as 16. Collect the rankings of the other members of your group and add them to your table. Add the figures across and fill in the column for the group's total ranking. the **lowest** total (nearest to 5) is the most important attribute, the next lowest the second most important attribute, and so on. What do your results reveal?

Management qualities identified by IMS report	Group member 1	Group member 2	Group member 3	Group member 4	Group member 5	Group's total ranking for each quality	Final order of importance for each quality
Communication							
Leadership							
Judgement							
Initiative							
Organisational skills							
Motivation							
Planning							
Innovation							
Good appearance							
Interpersonal skills							
Maturity							
Numeracy							
Adaptability							
Stress handling							
Personal energy							
Assertiveness							

I a) Did you generally agree or disagree as a group?

 b) Were there any attributes you all agreed or disagreed on?

2 Was anyone's ranking vastly different to the others?

3 Are there any attributes that you think are important which are not on the list?

---

66 DISCUSSION POINT 99

*W*hy would the attributes which are regarded as important vary from company to company?

Is there a typical manager?

Your answers to the activity ranking managers' qualities probably showed some agreement within your group about the most important qualities needed by managers. Does this mean, then, that there is a 'typical' manager?

The need for management to become a chartered profession was clearly stated by John Banham when he was CBI chief, at an annual conference of the Institute of Personnel Management. 'There is a misguided belief that management is nothing but applied common sense and the realm of the gifted amateur', he said, adding that, 'If we want to attract the most talented people into our business, management must become a profession with its own qualifications.' In other words, we need to have chartered managers as we have chartered accountants and chartered surveyors.

The concept of a chartered manager does, however, presume the existence of a universally accepted set of skills and knowledge. Certainly, the IMS report showed a great degree of consensus among the UK companies surveyed as to the qualities they looked for in managers. However, as Wendy Hirsh points out, the same terms can vary in meaning according to the company culture and job role of the manager. 'Good decision making in one company means taking innovative decisions, in another it means analysing hard data and minimising commercial risk.' The implication, therefore, is that skills gained in one company, which are closely related to the way things are done there, are not easily transferable to another company which is run on very different lines.

 In any case, as John Kotter of Harvard Business School points out in his book, *The Leadership Factor*, 'Figuring out the right thing to do in an environment of uncertainty caused by intense competitive activity and then getting others, often many others, to accept a new way of doing things demands skills and approaches that most managers simply did not need in the relatively calm 1950s, 1960s and early 1970s. It demands something more than technical expertise, administrative ability and traditional (especially bureaucratic) management. Operating in the new environment also requires leadership.'

What makes a leader?

Ask anyone about their idea of a leader and they would probably describe political figures such as Churchill, Martin Luther King and Mrs Thatcher or business leaders such as Richard Branson or Anita Roddick; leaders with such personal charisma they drew people to them like magnets and whose supporters wholeheartedly gave of their time, effort and commitment in following their leaders' goals. Famous examples such as these, which influence popular conceptions of what leaders are like, encourage most people to think that they could never aspire to being leaders themselves.

Yet most definitions view the essence of leadership as being the ability to motivate groups to achieve certain goals, without the use of any force or coercion. On this basis, many more people can be seen to function as leaders, though not perhaps with the same verve and dash as the truly inspirational figures. In fact, as firms today fight for survival in intensely competitive world markets, the need for leaders at all levels, not just at executive level, has never been greater.

Sir Michael Edwardes, the former chairman of BL (now Rover) cars, is quoted in Berry Ritchie and Walter Goldsmith's *The New Elite* describing the qualities he thinks good leaders have in common. 'They have this driving force inside them and people follow them because they inspire trust. They create confidence that they know what they are doing. The good leader is someone who is followed, rather than someone who obviously leads. People make the leader.'

Clearly leaders' influence stems from their acceptance by the group, and though this influence may often be reinforced by the power and authority conferred by their position within the organisation, acceptance is nevertheless not dependent on their formal status. In fact, any leaders who try and rely on their rank to command authority will never have more than a tenuous hold on their group. Respect must be earned, as it will not be automatically accorded by virtue of a person's job title or rank. Groups may reject a leader they do not respect, and if this happens they are likely to do the minimum required and may even work towards sabotaging the leader's efforts. Strong leadership is therefore essential if groups are to work productively.

In an interview with George Bickerstaffe of *Director* magazine, John Adair, the UK's leading authority on the subject, defines leadership as the control and integration of three elements – the task, the team and the individuals on the team. The role of the leader is therefore to motivate the individuals to come together as a team to complete the task in hand.

66 DISCUSSION POINTS 99

1 What are some of the characteristics of a good leader?

2 Can you think of any examples of strong, 'natural' leaders?

3 Do you agree with the old saying that 'leaders are born, not made'?

Is anybody worth over £1.5 million?

Table 8.1 *Executive salaries over £1,500,000*

Company	Executive	Total pay (inc bonus) £
SKB	Jan Leschly	8,045,330
BSkyB	Sam Chisholm	4,170,922
Lucas Varity	Victor Rice	4,102,658
Granada	Gerry Robinson	2,894,570
Rentokil Initial	Sir Clive Thompson	2,448,510
TI Group	Sir Christopher Lewinton	2,441,445
BAe	Sir Richard Evans	2,165,254
United News & Media	Lord Hollick	2,038,253
Zeneca	Sir David Barnes	1,875,544
Kingfisher	Sir Geoffrey Mulcahy CE	1,810,373
Pearson	Frank Barlow	1,781,538
Ladbroke	Peter George	1,561,885

Source: *The Sunday Times* 26.10.97, M. Lynn, R. Olins. 'Which of our bosses give the best value?' and other related articles from the same source.

The issue of 'fat cat' salaries (when executives are apparently paid excessive amounts) has been an issue for considerable debate in recent years. The amount earned by top executives is scrutinized carefully by the press, the government and employees. It is important to note that all of the above pay awards are agreed by the shareholders at the Annual General Meeting. As long as the shareholders (the owners) are satisfied with their own return, there tends not to be too much objection to such salaries. Total pay means salary plus bonuses, which can come in the form of share options. A share option allows the executive to sell an allocated number of shares at an agreed price – this is normally an incentive to increase the share price. When share options are 'exercised' (cashed in), this can increase the salary significantly. Recently, share options have been replaced with long-term incentive plans (LTIPs), meaning that executives will be clocking up bonuses that will only be paid at the start of the next millennium – a bright start for the next century!

DISCUSSION POINTS

1 Can any person's abilities be worth over £1,500,000 a year?

2 What impact can a good top executive have on a firm's fortunes?

3 Are high salaries needed to attract and keep top executives?

4 What other benefits might top executives receive?

Leaders or managers?

Leadership and management are very different roles and require very different people, according to Professor Abraham Zaleznik of Harvard Business School. Managers are essentially *administrators*, he believes, who motivate people to meet the company's objectives. Leaders, on the other hand, are *visionaries*, challenging existing practices and capable of motivating people to create and follow *new* objectives.

This does not imply that one role is more valuable than the other. The chief executive at the top obviously needs to exhibit leadership in the sense of having a clear long-term vision of where the company is going, yet may not always be good at administration. Managers at the operating level, however, tend to be better at administration and managing resources.

In any case, managers today, whether they are **line managers**, responsible for the running of a particular department or section, or **staff managers**, responsible overall for an administrative function like personnel, need increasingly to demonstrate leadership in order to motivate their groups towards greater performance.

As John Adair points out in the *Director* interview referred to above, people's expectations are

changing. 'People now look for a much higher level of leadership than before. They expect to be consulted; to be listened to; to be informed; to be kept in the picture; to be partners in the enterprise. Good leaders create that sense of being a team, of involvement and commitment.'

So how many of you could make good leaders? 'There's a lot talked today about charisma,' says John Adair, 'but the old definition of genius as 90 per cent perspiration and 10 per cent inspiration also holds true for leadership.' In other words, there is no substitute for hard work, energy and enthusiasm.

What does one of Britain's top chief executives look for in picking good people? Richard Giordano, non-executive chairman of The BOC Group, is quoted in *The New Elite* as stressing that 'You pick people by looking back at their records first of all . . . The second element I have learned the hard way. Make certain you pick people with a good set of personal qualities. I've had people who were probably intellectually below the salt. I've chosen employees who have been excessively defensive, bordering on dishonesty. They can't stand to see their mistakes in the light of day and have covered them up. I've had people who were just not articulate – brainy and all that, but hell on wheels to communicate with . . . Then there are some who just don't want to work!'

CASE STUDY

Dixons – managing a service revolution

The importance of leadership can be seen clearly in the recent change of business strategy at Dixons, Britain's biggest electrical retailer. For most of the past 50 years, its leader has been Sir Stanley Kalms.

In 1948 Sir Stanley joined a one-store family business called Dixons. Today he is chairman of Dixons Group

Plc, with its annual turnover of over £2,000 million and almost 20,000 employees. This remarkable growth stemmed from many causes. At the strategic level, the key was focus upon the pursuit of clear, demanding profit targets. In terms of day-to-day operations, success rested largely upon the firm's deal-making skills – both with suppliers and with customers. The company's sales success was based on financial incentives to store staff (through commission) and a training focus on clinching a sale.

By the late 1980s, however, there was increasing evidence that this might not be enough. Customers were looking for more than just the right products at the right price. They wanted better, quicker and more responsive service. As Helen Irving, Dixons' personnel director, says: 'Products are so complex nowadays. Customers want advice from well-informed staff and expect support following their purchase – preferably from the person they dealt with in the store'.

The prime mover in making service a top priority was Sir Stanley. In 1995 he set up a new executive committee called the Quality Standards Committee, in which he takes a keen interest. This sent out a message to all staff about its importance. Customer service would be the focal point of the company's strategy for the year 2000.

The new strategy would be three-pronged: investment in new service initiatives such as next-day delivery (including Sundays); a change in staff attitudes in favour of a greater customer focus; and partnerships with suppliers to identify and deliver the product quality improvements sought by customers. Within the stores, the need was to encourage staff to take an interest in all their customers' needs. This led to a service strategy called 'My Customer, My Responsibility' (MCMR). This would not be a simple task. The Dixons growth story had been rooted in staff focus on selling. Might a shift in emphasis undermine the company's turnover and profits? Or might sales staff only pay lip-service to their responsibility for customer service?

Helen Irving was sure that the answer was not just to retrain staff. A few days' training could not be expected to change attitudes. More important was to ensure that all 20,000 employees received a consistent message about the importance of service and their personal responsibility for providing it.

To help provide the consistent message, a Quality Standards director was appointed in September 1995 – answerable directly to the chairman. Adam Smith sees his job 'as being the customer champion'. Adam is clear that this is no less businesslike a job than any other in the company, because 'we didn't come to it from a moral point of view, we just want to be better than the competition'. So Adam has built on the change in staff attitude brought about by 'my customer my responsibility' with service initiatives such as Sunday delivery and 'service excellence week'. This helps turn Sir Stanley's aims into customer reality, with the likely long-term benefit of more loyal customers.

Yet would even these initiatives be enough? Customer service demands change constantly, so the company needs to spot new trends before the competition. And how can the company make sure that the customers from all its stores are equally happy with the service they receive?

A long-term solution is to provide a system for measuring service success. Dixons already had a measurement system called 'complaints against turnover' (CAT). This was calculated by dividing the number of customer complaints by the store's sales turnover. The lower the number, the better. This made it possible to produce a monthly league table of performance.

Customer complaints were not the only issue. A customer might leave a store feeling dissatisfied with the service, yet do nothing more than walk across the road to a competitor. So the hunt was on for a new way of measuring service performance. A set of customer satisfaction methods have been put in place to measure improvements to customer service over time, and to identify problems requiring immediate attention.

Head Office initiatives are all very well, but do they really affect what happens at local level? Not always, to be sure. In this case, though, the consistent messages from the company's leadership have ensured action. To Joe Earle, manager of the Curry's Superstore at Slough, the 'My Customer, My Responsibility' initiative has been important for its message to staff, rather than the systems it has introduced. It has encouraged individuals to take more personal responsibility for what they do and focused attention on service rather than sales. 'Take this customer complaint, for example', he continues. 'It was the only one we had last week, but my area manager has phoned this morning to ask about it. That would never have happened in the past.' He also cites service initiatives such as same-day delivery and installation. 'We used to just deliver a cooker to someone's door. They had to install it. That's all changed, which is great for the customers.'

Joe Earle with a member of staff and a customer

Julie Smith makes sales of over £1 million a year at Curry's, Slough. Her reward is a 1 per cent commission, but her motivation is 'to provide the standard of service I expect when I go anywhere'. Recently a customer phoned to ask about the length of the electrical lead and waste pipe on a dishwasher. Others would say they didn't know. Julie unfurled the items, measured them and phoned the customer back. The sale was made.

Joe Earle is also clear that the changes will help, not hinder, long-term profitability. He has no doubt that top-class service is the basis of high sales. At the Slough Superstore, 'my top salesperson gets the most customer praise – service and sales go hand in hand.'

Successful leadership, then, requires three elements: a clear vision of what is required; selecting the right people with enough power to deliver the vision; and providing the resources to finance a plan that turns the vision into practical changes which staff believe in.

ACTIVITY

1 You have £300 and want to buy a new midi sound system. Identify the factors you would consider before deciding what to buy and where to buy it. List six of each and then place them in order of priority.

2 Imagine you are the manager of a PC World Superstore. How would you make sure that your sales staff give excellent customer service? Try to think of at least eight methods.

What should management training include?

According to a report published in 1987, 'The Making of Managers', whose principal author was Professor Charles Handy, the extent of management training in the UK lags far behind that of its four main competitors.

The USA invests vast amounts in training; Japan has a compulsory system whereby managers have to go through a systematic process of self-education; in France, employers are required by law to spend a minimum annual sum on training for each employee; and the Germans go through a long preparatory training and normally do not even start their managerial careers until they are at least 27 years old.

What should a good management training programme include? Sir Trevor Holdsworth, the former chairman of GKN, has reservations about some of the courses at management training centres being too academic. He is quoted in *The New Elite* as arguing (jokingly) that the best management training course would be one confined to three disciplines: chess, bridge and poker. 'Chess represents strategic thinking in a wider form, while bridge is working with a partner and poker is taking a calculated risk and having the nerve to see it through. All the elements of business management are captured in those three games.'

Apart from the courses run at business schools and management training centres, many UK companies do in fact offer their own training courses.

How do management styles vary?

The degree to which a manager gives responsibility for decision making can be ranked along a scale, as shown in the diagram below.

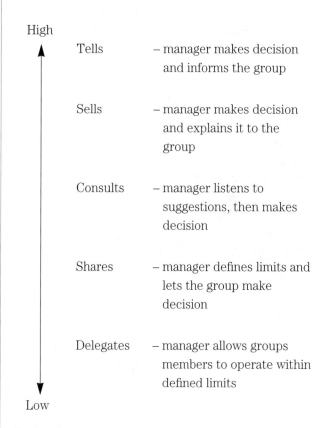

High

Tells — manager makes decision and informs the group

Sells — manager makes decision and explains it to the group

Consults — manager listens to suggestions, then makes decision

Shares — manager defines limits and lets the group make decision

Delegates — manager allows groups members to operate within defined limits

Low

Scale of management styles

Source: Tannebaum and Schmidt, *Harvard Business Review*.

At either end of the scale are the two styles of management – autocratic and democratic.

● **Autocratic** managers set objectives for the group, demonstrate their own authority, and expect orders to be obeyed blindly and without question. Communication is downward, so group members do not have the necessary information to make their own decisions. Such managers see workers as replaceable production units who can only be motivated by fear or by appeals to their self-interest in terms of money.

- **Democratic** managers, on the other hand, encourage group members to set their own objectives and delegate authority wherever possible, giving reasons for any orders or instructions they give out. Participation in decision making is encouraged and group members are given the necessary information to form these opinions, which the manager takes into account when making a final decision. This managerial style is based on workers being seen as human beings, who can be trusted to put their hearts into the task.

Research has shown that this last style results in the highest productivity, greatest feelings of involvement and job satisfaction and the best relations, though it does mean managers have to be good communicators and have to take time for the necessary consultation with workers.

However, a job-centred autocratic management style can also achieve high productivity, though groups managed like this tend to show dissatisfaction with their work and output is generally of lower quality. Such groups also experience greater conflict with management and suffer from a high turnover.

In any case, much research has also shown that managers do not adopt one style in all situations. The style adopted varies according to the manager's own personality, ability and experience and the personalities, skill and experience of the group members. The size of workforce, kind of job done and time available for completion are also influential. The nature of the organisation and the management style which have traditionally been used are important factors too.

ACTIVITY

Comparison of management styles

I Decide which type of management style would be most appropriate in the following situations:

a) A group of unskilled workers engaged in completing a complex task.

b) A group of inexperienced workers meeting a tight time deadline.

c) A new manager appointed to run a division of a large firm, where consultative committees have traditionally existed.

d) A group of skilled workers making high-quality products.

e) A group of skilled employees in a small family firm.

f) A large factory with hundreds of employees, when a fire breaks out.

g) A new manager taking over an ailing company who needs to cut production costs, reduce staff and introduce financial controls.

h) A group of inexperienced workers who believe management is paid to make decisions.

2 Why could you make a case for either style being appropriate in the situations in **g)** and **h)**?

DISCUSSION POINTS

1 Can one management style work best in most situations?

2 Which styles have been adopted by successful leaders that you can think of?

Management structures

Most companies have traditionally been organised on a **pyramid structure**, where employees at each level in the hierarchy are at a certain rank and have a particular role to fulfil in the organisation. In this kind of structure, there is a clearly defined **chain of command**. Orders tend to move downwards and the main flow of information is upwards.

At ICI a very steep pyramid existed, where it was calculated that there were as many as 16 layers of management between the shop floor and the chairman. As part of his recovery strategy for ICI, Sir John Harvey-Jones pruned out many of these layers in order to revitalise the management structure.

Some companies are now organised instead on a **matrix structure**, where the authority for decision making is shifted down the organisation so that it lies with the heads of sections or of subsidiary companies, giving them more autonomy. Even a business organised on a traditional pyramid structure may use the matrix approach at times, when complex problems need to be solved quickly. For example, a team of people spanning different areas like production, personnel, finance and marketing, drawn

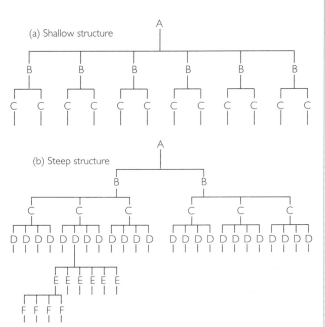

Pyramid organisational structure

from all levels in the organisation, may meet together to investigate a problem like poor quality control. A matrix structure such as this improves communication, speeds up decision making and encourages motivation through allowing employees greater opportunities for involvement and participation.

Who makes decisions?

How is authority for decision making actually allocated in different organisations? In organisations with a **centralised management structure**, the majority of decisions are made by a few people. Those with a **decentralised management structure**, on the other hand, may give responsibility for decision making to senior managers in different divisions concerned with different product groups. Such a shifting or **delegation** of responsibility for decision making downwards through the organisation encourages greater motivation, because of the autonomy gained.

A spectacular example of a company trying to shake itself free of head office bureaucracy occurred when Bob Horton, the former chairman of BP, was first appointed to the post. Within a week he announced that more than 1,000 jobs would be cut from BP's massive headquarters in the City. With them went an elaborate hierarchical structure and about 70 committees, all supposedly needed to manage or coordinate the global business, but which were actually stifling initiative and action in the operating units.

Peters and Waterman highlighted the fact that the successful American companies they studied invariably split their operations into small, independent units. Each unit is allowed maximum freedom to operate except in certain key areas, which management feel are so important that they need centralised control over them.

In their description of 23 successful British companies which they identified as standing out from the crowd, Walter Goldsmith and David Clutterbuck, in their book, *The Winning Streak*, found decentralised management structures were the norm. The only exceptions were the retailing chains and the Trust House Forte hotel chain, where a greater degree of central control is required to maintain uniform standards.

In describing the situation at Clarks, who operate in the shoe making industry, Goldsmith and Clutterbuck point out that 'The revelation came during the Second World War, when the company had to give up its main factory for the production of torpedoes. The mass production halls were dispersed into numerous smaller buildings in the surrounding area. Productivity rose 250 per cent. Since then, Clarks has retained all its production in relatively small, semi-autonomous units.'

These authors also observe that the basic philospohy behind the success of the Racal Electronics Group is their policy of establishing small individual companies, with less than 500 employees, each responsible for the design, development and marketing of its own products. According to Sir Ernest Harrison, the former chairman of Racal Electronics, 'A small business has one product and a small team of people, who can be so intense in their interest that they get the best product and the best effort out of the people who work for them. . . . Everyone knows the costs, everyone knows the boss and everyone knows the customers.'

CASE STUDY

Virgin – effective management in action

——

Pick up any newspaper or magazine and there's a good chance you'll come across a picture of Richard Branson sporting his irrepressible toothy grin and trademark woolly jumper. Airline owner, daredevil stunt man and entrepreneur extraordinaire, few businessmen have captured the public imagination as completely as the larger-than-life chairman of Virgin. The press have elevated him to the status of folk hero, reporting his hot-air balloon and speedboat exploits with relish and devoting endless column inches to each new business venture.

Branson's earliest business venture was in fact as the publisher of a student magazine when he was still a 16-year-old schoolboy. However, the real break came when, in a bid to raise cash for the financially-strapped magazine, he hit on the idea of selling discounted records by mail order. The initial advertisement produced a flood of responses and he was soon able to open his first Oxford Street record shop in 1971. The purchase of a recording studio in 1972 proved a huge success when the first album released – Tubular Bells by Mike Oldfield – went on to sell five million copies. At the age of 23, Branson had made his first million. In the years since, artists like Janet Jackson, Culture Club, the Human League, Phil Collins and Paula Abdul helped to turn the music division into one of the most successful record labels in the world. Branson later pulled off the deal of a lifetime when the sale of Virgin Music to Thorn EMI in 1992 netted the company a cool £560 million.

In the space of 25 years Branson has built a major entertainment empire with a turnover of £1.4 billion and 7,500 employees in 150 operating companies. Virgin interests around the world, as they are now, consist of five holding companies: Travel, Retail, Communications, Hotels and Investments. The two major divisions are Virgin Travel, which is dominated by the airline, and Virgin Retail which operates music and entertainment stores, including the Megastores chain. So what are the management principles governing the company whose growth has been almost entirely self-generated, with only a handful of acquisitions and partnership deals?

Branson's management philosophy rests squarely on the 'small is beautiful' principle put forward by the economist EF Schumacher. According to Schumacher, it is only when a large organisation is broken down into many small autonomous units, that the proper balance between freedom, which promotes creativity, and order, which gets things done, can be maintained. As Branson says, 'Once people stop knowing the other people in the building, it's time to break up a company into smaller units.

The ideal size is around 50 to 60 people. By keeping a company small, you give more people a chance.'

In line with this philosophy, the highly decentralised management structure that has evolved at Virgin is a classic example of 'empowerment', with managers being given the freedom to organise the day-to-day running of their companies as they see fit. As one manager points out, 'He'll sometimes disagree with you but then says, "Go ahead, you're the boss".' The fact that many of the top executives have been with the company since it started is perhaps the best proof that managers appreciate being given the room to follow their own judgement.

Staff turnover is also low. So what factors explain this loyalty? 'We're an entertainment company so things are done slightly differently to other companies', admits Branson. 'We don't have a clock-in, clock-out mentality. Because of this climate, people are quite willing to work long hours.' Based on the principle that people feel more motivated when they have a stake in the company's future, 85 per cent of promotions are internal appointments. Other key factors include the use of incentive payment schemes and the fact that employees have the option of buying shares in the company. In fact, well over a dozen of the top managers at Virgin are now millionaires in their own right.

Branson has clearly fostered a winning management style at Virgin, delegating authority to his managers whilst leaving himself free to do what he does best – coming up with ideas for new ventures and getting them off the ground.

Richard Branson

ACTIVITY

Jinx Games Ltd: 'all in a day's work!'

BACKGROUND TO THE COMPANY

Jinx Games Ltd is a manufacturer of board games, located in the small town of Daleford in the Pennines. The company employs 40 people, has a turnover of £1.8 million and is regarded locally as a reputable and well-run firm. Sales are seasonal and the firm gets especially busy in the run-up to Christmas. The company gets orders steadily from small toy shops round the country, but their biggest orders tend to be from the major department stores in the cities.

The firm was started eight years ago by Helen Robinson, who is the managing director. On this particular Friday in September, Helen arrives in the office at 10.30 a.m., after a meeting with one of the suppliers, to find on her desk a list of phone messages from her secretary together with a letter which arrived this morning. She also has a list of things written down in her diary to deal with today.

DECIDING PRIORITIES

Put yourself in the position of Helen Robinson. Having read the phone messages, letter and diary entries, decide how **urgent** and how **important** each situation is.

1 Make a list of the order in which you have to deal with each situation. (Plan the possible combinations in rough first.)

2 By the side of each item on your list, state which managerial role you are carrying out in dealing with each situation. (Refer back to the diagram of roles identified by Mintzberg on p.92.)

DALEFORD FOOTBALL CLUB

127 The Links
DALEFORD
OF7 2AL

Mrs Helen Robinson   September 9th
Jinx Games Ltd.
DALEFORD
DF3 4BH

Dear Mrs Robinson,
    We will be holding our annual
disco at the end of next month at
8.30 p.m. on October 28th.
    As you have very kindly
sponsored us this year, we wondered
if you would come along and present
the cups to the winning players?
I look forward to hearing from you.

Yours sincerely,

Kenneth Jameson

Kenneth Jameson
(Club Secretary)

PHONE MESSAGE

1. Factory foreman rang. Would like an interview to discuss his prospects in the company. Has had another job offer and needs to give them an answer by next weekend.

2. Finance controller rang. Customer owing £20,000 gone into receivership. He thinks another consignment of goods is to be dispatched today.

3. Reporter from 'Derbyshire Business Review' rang. Would like an interview for an article in next week's issue.

4. Buyer from Jarrods department store rang. Goods due to be delivered a week ago not arrived yet.

ACTION REQUIRED   Friday September 13th

1. Write memo informing everyone the company Christmas 'do' will this year be held at ' Marco and Luigis' on December 15th.
2. Arrange to see 'Platt and Margate' insurance brokers to update insurance policies which will run out at the end of the month.
3. Look at budget figures to decide where the money for advertising the new game to be launched in two months time is to be drawn from.
4. Ring 'Apollo Computers' to arrange for a representative to visit and discuss the computerisation of the company accounts system.
5. Arrange meeting with Sales Manager to review last month's sales figures.

Growing businesses

Introduction: the small firms revival

How small is small? Definitions vary, from the 'under 24 employees' stated by the Small Business Research Trust, to the measure adopted by the Department of Employment, which classifies small firms in manufacturing as being those with fewer than 200 employees. However, an accepted formula seems to be that described in the 1981 Companies Act. This defines a small firm as being one which during any accounting year does not exceed *two* of the following criteria: a turnover of £1.4 million, total assets of £0.7 million, a workforce of 50 employees.

The 1993 *Size Analysis of UK Businesses* showed that 89 per cent of all manufacturing firms are small firms of under 50 employees, accounting for 24 per cent of manufacturing employment. In fact, 66 per cent of all manufacturing firms were very small firms of under nine employees. Only 3 per cent of manufacturing firms have more than 200 employees!

In the post-war period of economic growth, small businesses were widely regarded as being inefficient. Only large firms could afford to adopt all the latest technological developments and improve their productivity by making huge economies of scale. The impact of such attitudes was confirmed by the government-commissioned Bolton Report, published in 1971, which concluded that, 'The small firms sector is in a state of long-term decline.' However, the report argued that small firms (which they defined as having fewer than 200 employees) fulfilled an important role in the economy, by creating jobs and stimulating competition and innovation. Some of the measures recommended by the report, such as the setting up of a Small Firms Service, were later adopted.

Since 1971, there has been a dramatic increase in the numbers of small firms. Why is this so? What advantages do small firms offer over larger firms? The UK's SMEs (small and medium enterprises) are estimated to have accounted for two-thirds of private sector employment and 75–100 per cent of net job creation in recent times, whereas during the 1980s the larges companies reduced their collective workforce by over 1.3 million. Unlike large firms, which are tending to shed jobs, small firms are creating jobs and thus stimulating economic growth.

In addition, their small scale of operations means that they do not face the same problems as larger firms, many of which are associated with production-line work. Due to their closeness to the market, they also tend to be more in touch with market trends. They can be more flexible in responding to changing market demands, because they are owner managed and so decisions can be taken quickly. They generally tend to be more innovative and, because they often provide highly specialised products and services, are seen as being important in providing consumers with a greater choice.

Apart from the advantages inherent in their small size, there are various economic, social and political factors which have encouraged the small firms revival.

Why do some industries have many small firms?

Richard Scase and Robert Goffee, in their book, *The Real World of the Small Business Owner*, describe four conditions which encourage small manufacturing firms to grow up. These include:

- **Labour intensiveness**. The textile, footwear and printing and publishing industries provide many opportunities for small firms. They are all traditional industries that depend on most work being done by hand rather than by machine.
- **Subcontracting**. The engineering industry sustains large numbers of small firms, who survive by supplying the specialised goods and services which large firms subcontract out.

TABLE 9.1 *Why are there more small firms today?*

Service industries	As the service sector of the economy has increased dramatically in recent years, more opportunities have been created for small firms. Service firms, being labour intensive, can be started with very little capital outlay, unlike manufacturing firms which need heavy initial outlays on plant and equipment.
Standards of living	More small firms are starting up as general standards of living have risen. These have exploited new markets catering for the specialised products and services demanded by consumers with higher disposable incomes.
Redundancies and unemployment	Many of the workers made redundant as a result of their firms closing down or cutting back have decided to start up small firms, especially if they live in areas where their chances of finding another job are slim. Similarly, many unemployed people have decided to set up their own businesses, as an alternative to the dole queues.
Opportunities for subcontracting	Large firms prefer to subcontract out limited production runs or specialised services where the work is not profitable for their scale of operations. This creates opportunities for small firms to survive in the **sheltered market** created. Opportunities increase in times of fierce competition, which causes large firms to concentrate even more on their core or principal activities.
Government encouragement	Small firms are widely recognised as creating jobs, stimulating economic growth and avoiding many of the labour problems larger firms face. As a result, most governments have actively encouraged the formation of small firms in recent decades.

- **Technological innovation**. The plastics, instrument engineering and electronic engineering industries are all areas where small firms have grown up making the innovative products which have been developed.
- **Market variability**. The furniture and clothing industries and the manufacture of various domestic items are all consumer goods industries which offer **market niches** for new businesses, catering for particular fashions or specialised items.

Of these factors, Scase and Goffee conclude that 'labour intensiveness is perhaps the most important since the initial capital requirements for start up purposes tend to be low'.

Why do people set up in business?

Becoming an **entrepreneur** involves undertaking a risk in a commercial venture. What factors motivate the ever increasing flood of people to risk going it alone? The 'Enterprise in Britain' study of almost 6,000 small business owners and self-employed people showed that the age at which most people start up is between 30 and 40, when they have the work experience, access to capital (with mortgages easier and children growing up) and necessary motivation (if promotion does not materialise).

Dissatisfaction with being an employee is undoubtedly the trigger for many, especially if there is no challenge or job satisfaction left in their present jobs and prospects of promotion are limited. Running a business can provide an attractive alternative to being stuck on the company ladder, with the opportunity to make decisions, take on responsibility and enjoy what is for many entrepreneurs the main benefit – the ability to control their own destiny. Some employees may decide in time to put their skills and abilities to use making profits for themselves, rather than for the organisation they

have been with. Those who are at a disadvantage in the labour market because of discrimination, such as ethnic minority groups, also find business start-ups attractive.

Similarly, according to Robert Goffee and Richard Scase in their book *Women in Charge*, a growing number of women are starting their own businesses to avoid the frustration of limited career prospects. 'To a large extent this is because senior male managers continue to query their ability to occupy top corporate positions. Some are concerned about the supposed psychological and emotional qualities of women, others are anxious about their organisational "commitment". As a result, there may be a reluctance to train or promote women. By starting their own business women can achieve the material success and personal ambitions denied them in large organisations.'

People may also be tempted to become entrepreneurs through deciding to develop an innovative idea for a product or service that they have come up with, but which their present company does not regard as commercially viable. David Oates, in his book *The Complete Entrepreneur*, quotes the case of Robert Mann, who stumbled on an idea for a fire protection product he was sure would sell well. The product was based on a material which is inset as a thin strip in vulnerable areas such as door frames. If a fire occurs the material expands under the heat, sealing off the gap in the frames and preventing the fire spreading. The chemical group he was working for at the time thought the product was too specialised and was unlikely to generate a big enough sales volume to justify the necessary investment. However, the firm agreed to support him by supplying him with the raw material at a good price and also helped him with credit. Within just five years, Mann's company was exporting worldwide and had a turnover of £400,000.

In some cases, people have become entrepreneurs because they have discovered a gap or niche in a particular market through wanting to use a product or service, finding it does not exist and then deciding to manufacture or supply it themselves. Others seek to provide an existing product or service for a gap which they have identified in a local or regional market. Less often than is commonly thought, small businesses are founded by those who manage to invent a completely new product or service, thus stimulating a new demand. Sometimes entrepreneurs can discover a useful product which is not widely available and set up a company themselves to market it more extensively.

Changing personal circumstances, such as being made redundant, can often be a powerful spur, with the redundancy lump sum providing some of the finance needed. However, evidence suggests that businesses started by individuals who have been pushed into start-ups by negative reasons have a lower growth rate than businesses started by those who have become entrepreneurs for positive reasons, such as identifying a gap in the market or coming up with an idea for a new product.

The trend towards increasing numbers of **management buy-outs** in recent years shows no sign of slowing down. This is where the managers buy out the company they are working for, or a division of it, and then run it as an independent concern. The impetus for taking this step is often the threat of closure. Buy-outs have tended to be very successful, on the whole, largely because the management team who already have experience of running the company stays in place. Finance is easier to obtain for such ventures because they are already a going concern, so constitute less risk for investors than completely new start-ups.

Whatever the motivating factors, with the 'enterprise culture' that exists in Britain today and the degree of help and advice available, conditions for starting up a small business have never been more favourable. The first step for any new entrepreneur is to prepare a detailed business plan on all aspects of the proposed venture, in order to assess whether the idea is commercially viable.

ACTIVITY

Factors considered by a bank manager when assessing a business plan

The questions that follow are adapted from Barclays Small Business pack for small firms.

Which of the following factors do you think a bank manager would assess most carefully in a business plan?

- Background of entrepreneur
- Background of business
- Products or services
- Markets and sales
- Financial considerations
- When will break-even point be reached?
- Has the entrepreneur any relevant experience in this field?
- Have the strengths which make the business competitive in the market been identified?
- Can the repayments be met on the amount borrowed?
- What will happen if the key personnel are unable to work?
- Has a target market been identified?
- Are premises adequate for future needs?
- How much of his/her own capital is the entrepreneur prepared to put in?
- What are the entrepreneur's business objectives, and how practical are they?
- Have the core or principal products or services been identified?
- Is the level of projected sales realistic?

- Who are the key suppliers and how much trade credit will they allow?

- Is the choice of premises suitable, in terms of size, location and cost, for the type of business?

- What percentage does each product or service contribute to turnover?

- How will prices be calculated?

- Does the cash-flow forecast include a reasonable margin of error?

- Is the market declining, static or increasing, and why?

- How detailed is the breakdown of expenditure?

- Who are the major competitors?

- Is the cash-flow forecast realistic and detailed enough?

- Has the entrepreneur any recognised business training?

- Has any market research been carried out?

- Has the entrepreneur already got any firm orders?

- What methods of marketing will be used?

- What insurance cover will be taken out?

- Does the planned expenditure take into account future growth?

- Is the general character of the entrepreneur suitable for running a business?

- Can the business obtain any grants?

ACTIVITY

The lending quiz – how would a bank rate your business plan?

——

On your copy of the questions below, tick the answer which you think is most appropriate for each question. When you have finished, add up the scores given for each answer on the scoring sheet, to determine **your** credit rating.

1 You are writing your own business plan to apply for a bank loan to start up a small business. Do you:

   a) include a short paragraph outlining your background and career so far?

   b) include a detailed profile of yourself giving full details of your previous relevant experience, work achievements, training and education?

   c) leave out any details about yourself as this is less relevant than the sales projections and cash flow forecasts you have included?

2 You are able to raise as personal finance, through a variety of sources, a percentage of the start-up finance required. Do you contribute:

   a) 10 per cent?

   b) 20 per cent?

   c) 40 per cent?

3 You are assessing the likely size and nature of potential demand for your products. Do you:

   a) carry out an informal survey amongst friends and family?

   b) commission a well-known, reputable market research agency to carry out a detailed survey?

   c) obtain any previously published survey results for similar products and carry out some field research for a small sample?

4 You are deciding how to plan the marketing most efficiently. Do you:

   a) carry out test marketing in order to decide how to use adverts, leaflets etc. in a logical sequence?

   b) commission a well-known and reputable advertising agency to test-market your products?

   c) avoid wasting scarce start-up resources on test marketing, as you already know what products you want to sell and how you need to market them?

5 You are deciding which bank to approach for start-up finance. Do you:

a) approach a new bank as you think it is going to be more receptive than your own, giving them a complete set of bank statements for the last three years, showing satisfactory account behaviour?

b) approach your own bank with which you have banked satisfactorily for five years?

QUIZ SCORING SHEET

Add up your scores:

1 a) 4 marks	**3 a)** 2 marks	**5 a)** 4 marks
b) 8 marks	**b)** 2 marks	**b)** 6 marks
c) 2 marks	**c)** 6 marks	
2 a) 2 marks	**4 a)** 4 marks	MY SCORE:
b) 4 marks	**b)** 2 marks	MAX SCORE: 36
c) 8 marks	**c)** 8 marks	

CREDIT RATING

Final score

30 or more	Your loan application is certain to be approved as it is well prepared and thorough.
24–29	Your loan application is likely to be approved though some areas will need a bit more attention to detail.
18–23	You need to go away and prepare a more carefully thought-out business plan if you wish the application to go through.
Under 18	You need to think again about whether there is any point in your going into business on your own.

Raising the finance to start up

Most entrepreneurs struggle hard to raise the start-up capital needed for all the one-off purchases like machinery or premises, together with the working capital needed to pay for everyday running costs such as a stock of materials, wages, overheads and so on. Though preoccupied with survival and trying to keep their heads above water, their thoughts might occasionally stray to the day when their business takes off to the point where it starts to make millions and becomes a major household name. Just a pipe dream? Perhaps, yet the dream does become a reality for some.

The founding of Apple, the US-based computer firm, illustrates the kind of rags-to-riches success story which inspires many hard-pressed entrepreneurs to keep going when they might otherwise be tempted to give up. In common with the majority of small business start-ups, Apple began life on a shoestring budget.

The company was founded in 1977 by Steve Jobs and his partner Steve Wozniak. They began working from a garage, having sold some of their belongings to raise their start-up capital of $1,300. A shop owner liked their design drawings for the second version of their computer so much that he placed an order for 50 computers straight away. But this large order created problems because it meant they could not afford to buy the electronic parts they needed. In fact, they eventually obtained the $20,000's worth of parts needed from a supplier on a 30-day-trade credit basis – and managed to pay it all back in 29 days with the cash they got from the sale of the 50 computers.

However, things might well have gone wrong. If they had not been able to manufacture and deliver the computers within 30 days, or if the customer had been late paying them, the story might have been very different. In the event, the company went from strength to strength. Within the next four years, sales multiplied 430 times, according to one estimate.

Entrepreneurs generally have some of their own capital to invest, from savings, for instance, or a second mortgage on their home. Just how easy is it for small businesses to borrow money today? The high street clearing banks are by far the most important source of initial finance. They tend to have a reputation for being conservative, preferring safe rather than speculative investments – mainly because they are, after all, responsible to their own depositors, whose savings they are investing.

Most advances are based on the concept of shared risk, where only about 50 or 60 per cent of the capital required is lent. Investors want to see the entrepreneur put in the rest, partly as a gesture of good faith (if you are unwilling to risk your own money, why should they risk theirs?), and partly because they would expect even greater effort and commitment if some of the entrepreneur's own capital was at stake. This principle is also adopted in the government's **Enterprise Allowance Scheme**, where people who have been unemployed are given £40 a week for a year when they start up a business, conditional on them already having or being able to borrow £1,000 themselves.

Lenders also require security to recover their loan should the business fail, the **collateral** often being provided in the form of the entrepreneur's own home. The government's **Loan Guarantee Scheme** is useful because it enables a loan to be granted in situations where it might otherwise not be; for instance, where inadequate security or the lack of an established track record makes the proposition unattractive to lenders. The government guarantees 70 per cent (85 per cent in some inner city areas) of a loan made by banks or financial institutions, up to a maximum of £100,000, thus enabling small businesses to provide the security lenders require. The small firm pays a 2.5 per cent premium to the government for the guarantee, which adds to the cost of borrowing. The scheme is now administered by the Training and Enterprise Councils (TECs).

In addition, small businesses can obtain finance through schemes such as LINC. Run by 14 Enterprise Agencies, this is a nationwide business introduction service which functions essentially as a 'marriage service'. Details of the small firms seeking capital are published in a monthly bulletin and investors can contact the firms which interest them via the box numbers given. Small firms can also raise finance through the European Investment Bank (EIB), which advances funds to banks and financial institutions which then lend on to small businesses. In the UK, this loan arrangement is carried out by Barclays Bank.

CASE STUDY

Braebourne Ltd – turning water into gold

‘On day one we borrowed a van and went down to fill 30 bottles in a spring in Devon. It took us two months to sell them!' Six years later, on 19 September 1996, William Record went down to the Savoy Hotel to pick up his prize at the 1996 Venturer of the Year Award. In the meantime, his business had grown to generate a profit of over a quarter of a million pounds a year.

It was while studying economics at Southampton University (he received a 2.1) that William Record started thinking about starting up on his own. 'Working for a huge company wasn't appealing' he says. Advice from his father pointed him towards rental businesses, because of their steady cash flow. 'My first thought was renting tropical plants to London offices . . . but the 1989 recession was starting . . . so it seemed unwise . . . then I came across water coolers.'

When he completed his degree he started researching the market for bottled water: 'I went through all the Mintel reports . . . we drank 2–3 litres per head compared with 25–30 in the U.S. . . . the growth rate in Britain was about 25 per cent a year . . . and there were more than 10 million water coolers in the States.' His mind was made up – the business would be renting water coolers to offices, delivering 22 litre bottles of natural mineral water to the customer with speedy and efficient service. He drew up a business plan, decided on the company and brand name 'Braebourne', and started up with £10,000 of share capital and a £25,000 loan from Lloyds Bank in February 1990.

Having collected the bottles of water from Devon, he and a friend started phoning everyone they knew, hoping for custom. They were offering a free 10 day trial with a free bottle of water. Selling proved very difficult. They tried visiting offices directly, but that proved a waste of time. Telephone selling ('telesales') using Business Directory numbers proved the best approach. Although it took two months to persuade the first 30 customers to try the free offer, 60 per cent of them converted into regular renters. Slowly, the business was starting to take off.

By early May, though, William realised the business was running out of cash. Every sales success was at a huge cost in wasted telephone calls and mailings. And every sale meant buying a water cooler for cash, then paying extra to deliver and install it. These cash outflows should have been offset by cash in from sales, but the free offer together with slow payments from customers caused the company's cash to drain away at an alarming rate.

Looking back, William thanks his father for the fact that 'from day one we had excellent management accounts, so we always knew where we were month by month'. As a result the cash crisis was anticipated. William hired an accountant to help draw up a revised, very full business plan, then went round the banks in search of capital. Remarkably, NatWest Bank gave Braebourne an overdraft of £80,000.

Shortly afterwards, William struck oil. The summer of 1990 was a beauty. Suddenly, instead of Braebourne staff phoning out, it was the incoming calls that had to be coped with. Demand soared as high as the temperatures. This, again, caused cash problems as more and more coolers had to be bought and staff hired. Even the water was running out! The demand was so high that the original Devon spring could not cope. So a new, larger spring was found in the Cotswolds. Braebourne coped with the summer only with the help of family loans to the tune of £30,000.

The key factor in the long-term future of the business was soon to be settled. What would happen when summer turned to autumn? Would the phone start to ring with customers cancelling their rentals? Fortunately, then and today, Braebourne's customer retention rate is 90 per cent. In other words the company loses only 10 per cent of customers per year. Bearing in mind that half of those are because of non-payment (i.e. Braebourne sack the customer) and some are due to office moves, the rate of loss due to customer disenchantment is very low indeed.

By Christmas 1990, the company's cash problems were heading for a new crisis. William recalls: 'We were really up against it . . . we considered leasing instead of buying coolers . . . and tried but failed to borrow money through the government's Loan Guarantee Scheme . . . then we went round the venture capital houses . . . they all turned us down because we were too small – we only wanted £100,000!'. Eventually 3i were persuaded of the company's strong growth prospects. Braebourne's capital was restructured, with the share capital increased to £50,000, of which £12,500 was to be held by 3i. In addition, 3i provided £106,000 of medium-term loans – an act of faith which encouraged NatWest to increase the overdraft to £100,000. From that day onwards, the involvement of 3i meant an end to the cash flow crises. When extra finance was needed, discussions with 3i led to further capital being made available. Today (February 1997) William feels confident that 'borrowing £1 million wouldn't be a problem'.

Since the frantic days of 1990 Braebourne has made huge progress. While the industry has been growing at 35 per cent a year, Braebourne has grown at 65 per cent to make it the third largest water cooler supplier in the U.K. In the year to January 1997 it made over £500,000 profit on net assets of £750,000. William has considered floating the business on the AIM stock market, but decided instead to keep the business growing until it is large enough for a full stock market listing.

Braebourne Ltd Profit/Loss

Despite the rapid growth, William has not seen a need to spread outside London and the South East. His principle is that every customer should be no more than an hour's drive from a Braebourne depot. So customer service is rapid and reliable and costs are kept down. Today there are three Braebourne depots, in the south, west and north of London. He believes his market share in London is about 12 per cent, so there is still plenty of growth potential.

So what has William learnt from the whole process? Looking back he feels that his main weakness was in marketing: 'If I'd done a marketing degree I'd have approached the whole thing more scientifically'. Today he has a team of eight telesales staff and two marketing graduates to provide accurate market research information and a fully costed marketing strategy. The company will spend £600,000 in 1997 on marketing, including advertisements on the London Underground, mailshots to personnel managers and to managing directors and a series of attractive brochures.

Another lesson has been focus. In 1993, slow sales in the winter encouraged William to start up a coffee machine rental business. In fact it proved a slow, relatively unprofitable distraction from the rapidly growing water market. Far more sensible has been the introduction in Autumn 1996 of water cooling machines which have an extra tap which delivers the water at just below boiling point. This provides a quick, easy way of making a cup of tea or coffee with mineral water – appealing and convenient for staff, and a great way of stimulating water sales in the winter.

The most important lesson to be learnt from William Record, though, is the fun he had on route to becoming successful. He recalls that: 'Starting your own business is like the first day of the summer holidays . . . It's exciting!'. He has also enjoyed the process of learning – from his own mistakes or from the people he has employed. There is no question of him sitting back and counting his money. William is already planning where Braebourne will be in three years' time.

An example of Braebourne's advertising on the London Underground

ACTIVITY

Ranking of ingredients of success in new ventures

On your individual copy of the table below, rank each ingredient of success in new ventures in order of importance from 1 to 10, and write the ranking in column 1. Rank the ingredient you rate as being most important as 1, through to the least important as 10. Collect the rankings of other members in your group and add them to your table. Add the figures across and fill in the column for the group's total ranking. The **lowest** total (nearest to 5) is the most important ingredient, the next lowest the second most important, and so on. What do your results reveal?

1 Did you generally agree or disagree, as a group?

2 Were there any ingredients of success that you all agreed or disagreed on?

3 Are there any factors that you think are important which are not on the list?

Ingredients of success in new ventures	Group member 1	Group member 2	Group member 3	Group member 4	Total ranking for group	Final order of importance
Having relevant experience of the industry.						
Identifying an unexploited gap in the market.						
Creating a new need by offering an innovative product or service.						
Catering for a specialised part of the market, rather than for the majority market.						

Ingredients of success in new ventures	Group member 1	Group member 2	Group member 3	Group member 4	Total ranking for group	Final order of importance
Directing marketing at the target market.						
Keeping overheads low in the early stages.						
Having enough cash to meet requirements for working capital						
Ensuring interest charges and loan repayments can be funded from profits.						
Applying for any grants available and seeking advice from outside agencies						
Diversifying early on to avoid overdependence on a few products.						

Raising the finance for growth

Research has shown that business start-ups are usually financed by a combination of personal finance, bank loans and overdrafts, obtained mainly from the high street banks. Business expansion, on the other hand, tends to be financed by reinvested profit. However, if a company continues expanding the profits which are ploughed back into the company may not be sufficient to fuel continued growth. An injection of **equity capital** may then be required. Equity is risk capital: the proprietor's own funds in the case of a sole trader or partnership, and share capital in the case of a limited company. Further equity can provide the funds required to pay for extra factory space and machinery, or for the higher wages and overheads resulting from expansion.

How easy is it to find risk capital, once a decision has been made that an injection of equity is needed?

Unfortunately, major investors prefer to invest their money in large public companies quoted on the Stock Exchange, which offer a lower risk than small businesses.

A worry about investing in a small firm is that success might lead to excessive expansion. A common cause of company failure is overtrading, meaning expanding so rapidly that cash outflows outstrip inflows, leaving the firm vulnerable to a shock such as a large bad debt.

Derwent Valley Foods Limited (Phileas Fogg) nearly went into liquidation in 1984. It doubled its factory size and hired new workers to cope with demand. This caused a major cash drain made worse by the failure of the accounting system to keep up with the increased level of business. Derwent asked the bank for an extra £200,000 overdraft, but the bank manager had lost confidence in the Derwent directors and refused. For several weeks the directors feared liquidation. Fortunately the regional director of the bank had attended Prince Charles's opening of the factory extension, and was willing to listen. Backed by 3i (Investors in Industry) and the Derwent directors, the extra overdraft was granted in November 1984.

In recognition of the problems of business expansion, the government's Enterprise Investment Scheme has been set up to encourage investment in small firms. Under the scheme, individuals are encouraged to invest between £500 and £100,000 in eligible companies (which are not quoted on the Stock Exchange). The incentives for them are that they can claim 20 per cent tax relief on their investment and pay no capital gains tax on any profit made. The investment must be maintained for at least five years.

Venture capitalists accept that a certain degree of risk is inevitable (as much as a one-in-three failure rate for start-ups). They tend not to be interested in investing below £50,000. They usually hold between 20 and 40 per cent of the company's shares and aim to recoup their investment when the company goes public, by selling the shareholding. Europe's leading venture capital company is 3i Group plc. They have helped over 11,000 firms since 1945 and currently have investments in over 3,200 companies.

CASE STUDY

Denby Pottery – a management buy-out success

———

Wedgwood, Denby and Royal Doulton are internationally famous for traditional English china and pottery. All three were established around two centuries ago, yet all have had dramatic, even traumatic, changes of ownership during the last 15 years.

For Denby, the drama started in 1987 when the company became one of many firms taken over by Coloroll plc. This fast growing, ambitious company allowed local Denby management to run the business and were keen to provide capital for investment. Yet the onset of recession in 1989 dragged Coloroll down, leaving Denby's fate in the hands of the receiver. A receiver's task is to raise as much as possible from asset sales, in order to repay creditors, so the directors knew that their business would soon be sold off.

The directors responded by proposing a management buy-out. They found experienced advisers who recommended 3i as financial backers. After 3i had checked the assets, trading position and cash-flow forecasts, the final issue was the personality fit. Could the 3i team work with the Denby managers? The answer was a resounding yes, so an agreement was reached.

Now the management buy-out (MBO) team could put together a detailed plan and offer to the receiver. A number of other companies were bidding to buy the business, so the Denby directors were pessimistic about their chance of success. Yet on 24 July 1990, the MBO team's bid of £5.3 million won the receiver's approval.

Denby was now an independent but potentially vulnerable small firm with large debts to its bankers. The four directors owned 60 per cent of the shares, with the remainder held by 3i.

The directors faced three main problems:

● The product range had become too large and diverse, making it hard for customers to develop a clear image of the Denby look and leading to short, uneconomic production runs.
● As Denby offered big profit margins to retailers, it had become common for Denby tableware to be displayed 'on sale, 33 per cent off' at many shops, threatening to cheapen Denby's image.
● In the 1970s, half of Denby's sales had been for export, but by 1990 this share had fallen to just 10 per cent, and the overseas distribution channels had withered away.

Denby was fortunate to have a managing director, Stephen Riley, whose career background was in marketing. Within the buy-out team he was responsible for marketing and product design and in a position to focus the business on these three problems.

The design team was encouraged to look for distinctive products of broad, international appeal, building on Denby's production strength of deep, rich glazes. This was to pay off with successful new product launches in each of the following years, culminating in 1994's award winning launch of Greenwich tableware. By 1995, 65 per cent of sales were stemming from products launched since the management buy-out.

Managing director, Stephen Riley, in the design studio at Denby Pottery

To tackle the image problem of retail discounting, Denby discussed the position with each of the major retail chains (such as Debenhams and House of Fraser). A three-year programme was agreed whereby the retailers accepted lower discounts in return for Denby's promise to invest in new, distinctive products. These would then be launched without promotional pricing.

The third element of the marketing strategy was to build export sales. The problem here would be the cost. Setting up a sales and distribution network in America, for example, might prove a hugely expensive flop. After an unsuccessful push in

Greenwich tableware

California, Denby decided to target the smaller, more receptive department store chains of middle America. This proved very successful, making it ever easier to find new US outlets willing to stock Denby. Sales in America more than doubled in 1994 alone and by 1995 Denby had more than one thousand American stockists. Europe is also being targeted, with France the stepping stone.

In addition to these strategic moves, the directors decided on two further marketing initiatives. Denby began to advertise regularly in magazines to emphasise the slogan 'Distinctively Denby'. There was also a substantial development of the factory shop into a varied and attractive Visitors Centre, including a full factory tour. This now has more than 250,000 visitors a year, and has turned from a promotional device into a profit centre in its own right.

With sales on a strongly upward path, the directors' attention needed to turn to production. How could the firm ensure sufficient output to meet customer demand? Raw materials presented no problem, as the pottery is built into the side of the hill where the clay was found nearly two centuries ago. More staff could,

TABLE 9.2 *Denby's financial progress 1990–94*

	1992	*1993*	*1994*	*1995*	*1996*	*1997*
Sales turnover (£000)	12,484	17,563	21,915	25,795	33,120	36,480
Operating profit (£000)	1,588	3,243	4,550	4,941	6,390	7,180
Profit margin (profit as percentage of sales)	12.7	18.5	20.8	19.2	19.3	19.7
Pre-tax profit (£000)	1,261	2,755	4,130	4,762	6,080	6,630

Source: Denby Pottery Plc, 1997

and would, be hired, but the kilns were already in operation 24 hours a day, so extra capital investment was required.

Two new tunnel kilns were installed at a cost of £580,000, each capable of firing pottery at the 1,200 degrees centigrade required for Denby's glazing process. A further £7 million was spent on up-to-date machinery such as a Japanese plate-making machine that uses a microwave drying process to speed up production. Happily, this huge investment has not been at the cost of jobs. With production volume more than doubling between 1990 and 1995, 200 more jobs have been created.

By 1994, with substantial progress on all fronts, the directors decided to float Denby on the stock market. This would raise extra capital for the business and enable the buy-out team to sell some shares. In May 1994, the shares were offered to the public at 130p, which placed a market value of £43 million on the business. This made all four directors multimillionaires, and gave 3i a substantial profit on its investment. On 2 June 1994 shares in The Denby Group Plc began trading on the London Stock Exchange.

Looking back, Stephen Riley can see that the four were lucky to have had the opportunity to buy out a run-down but profitable company, largely financed by borrowed money. Hindsight makes the directors' success look easy. In fact, the four pushed ahead with the MBO to save their own jobs and families, and those of their staff. It was not obvious in the midst of the 1990 recession that the new Denby would necessarily survive, let alone thrive.

Now, with the original shareholders still owning 40

per cent of the shares, and the team's sights set on a trebling of export sales by the year 2000, the future for Denby's 680 staff looks secure.

CASE STUDY

Dyson – how PricewaterhouseCoopers reduced the odds

O ver the past five years, James Dyson has become a household name through his invention of a bagless vacuum cleaner which maintains 100 per cent suction 100 per cent of the time.

His autobiography *Against the Odds* tells the story of the struggle James faced, and which many businesses face, seeking finance for the development of an idea or a new product.

James came up with an idea to change vacuum cleaner technology for the better while vacuuming at home one Saturday. He realised his bag cleaner

Dyson vacuum cleaner

kept losing suction, because the dust it sucked up actually clogged the pores of the paper bag through which air had to pass in order to create the suction. By replacing the bag with a cyclone system, which spins dirt and air and separates one from the other by centrifugal force, James overcame this problem of the bag clogging.

However, the initial reaction to his idea was one of doubt; financial backers insisted that had there been a better type of vacuum cleaner possible, then one of the multinational competitors would have invented it.

Despite this initial reaction, James Dyson produced 5,127 vacuum cleaners over a period of four years at home, in order to perfect his Dual Cyclone system. He then decided that licensing his product was the best way to see it put into production, so travelled the world looking for licensees. James was successful in gaining licence agreements in Japan and the USA, but was still convinced that he could achieve a significant market share, perhaps on home ground, by manufacturing the vacuum cleaner himself.

He approached a variety of venture capitalists and banks, confident that he could persuade them to back the investment on three counts:

● the success of his licence agreements for vacuum cleaners in Japan

● a highly detailed database available through his would-be distributors

● a successful track record in similar design-oriented businesses, e.g. the ball barrow

Every time he approached a bank he was met with the same reaction. Such institutions did not seem convinced that James, as a designer, would be able to manage a business well. Despite his past success in running companies, they still demanded considerable financial investment from James; something he was not in a strong position to give, having spent so much on design and development over the previous 12 years. This is a typical Catch-22 situation faced by many businesses. Providers of finance will only lend when there is either sufficient security in the form of assets, such as houses, or a solid trading record and

obvious potential for sales. The problem was exacerbated by the fact that at the time there was a recession which negated the opportunity for a share issue.

James raised the amount required to start production in the UK by selling the production licence in Japan (terminating any future cash flows in terms of licence fees) and he also managed to persuade Lloyds bank to lend sufficient further capital to get the project started.

Orders had already been placed, based on James' demonstrations with his prototype, and production began in Chippenham in 1993. In 1995, Dyson Appliances moved to a purpose-built factory at Malmesbury, Wiltshire, having rapidly outgrown its Chippenham premises.

Table 9.3 *Revenue of Dyson Appliances, 1994–1997*

Year	Revenue (£)
1994	3m
1995	40m
1996	100m
1997	150m

During the same period of time, the number of staff employed increased from 12 to 1,000

Although the business was now set-up and manufacturing, James had to be careful to ensure a positive cash flow. When businesses expand quickly (see table 9.3) there are dangers of running out of cash for the following reasons:

1 Sales need to be given on credit as a form of sales promotion.
2 Suppliers require instant cash (the business represents a potential risk because it has no trading record).
3 Wages are paid weekly.
4 Stocks are needed for a higher level of sales, whilst the cash coming in from present sales revenue is lower than the stock figures, due to growth.
5 When goods are being produced, money is 'tied up' in stock, i.e. not being sold and providing cash.
6 Marketing expenses need to be paid in cash until the business has established itself.

Ironically, once the business began trading, cash flow problems disappeared. Suppliers realised that the business was safe to trade with and worked on a 30 days credit period. The business avoids the problem of stock by holding only one or two days' worth of output in the factory. The fundamental solution to all cash flow problems may lie in the pricing strategy: Dyson products have a quality and efficiency which allowed them to have a price point which, at the start of trading, was around double the price of other vacuum cleaners on the market. James Dyson's idea worked on the theory that consumers would be willing to pay a premium price for a product which made vacuuming easier and better in the home. They were already paying higher prices for goods such as trainers and tennis rackets, so why not for vacuum cleaners? Furthermore, such a profit margin has allowed further expansion and investment into research and development, all of which has been funded from retained profit.

As the business grew, so the support and IT systems grew to match. The advice of Price Waterhouse, a large partnership of accountants and the group's financial auditors, was sought for 'best practice'. Contrary to popular myth, accountants perform a multiplicity of business advisory roles, rather than just dealing with numbers. Price Waterhouse helped to advise on the correct route for establishing overseas subsidiaries in France, Germany, Australia and other European countries. Tax and foreign exchange planning became more important to the group, as did the need to recruit high-calibre staff who could manage a large and growing organisation.

Price Waterhouse also sponsors a competition to encourage entrepreneurial skills called the 'West of England Business of the Year Award'. Dyson was a finalist in 1996 and won the competition in 1997 – James believes this competition forced the business into self-appraisal and consequently helped it to develop.

Three of the many lessons to be learned from this case study, which are very dear to James Dyson himself, are:

1 Manufacturing should not be seen as a dirty word, but as a creator of wealth (see Introduction chapter).
2 Design is not just about how something looks – rather how it works.
3 Businesses need good ideas, products and financial advice.

Source of data: Interview with James Dyson 10/2/98

 DISCUSSION POINTS

1 What is the danger of banks continually refusing to lend money?

2 What would Dyson Appliances need to consider if one day it decided to float on the Stock Exchange?

3 Discuss why trainers and tennis rackets are similar to Dyson Appliances' vacuum cleaners.

Business integration

IN ASSOCIATION WITH

Unilever

What is integration?

In today's business climate, competition is intense in almost every market you can possibly think of. Consequently, companies are constantly looking for ways to improve their competitive advantage or to increase their market share. This can be achieved by a process of **integration**, which is the joining of two companies.

One benefit of integration is related to savings due to the increased size of the business. Savings can be made in marketing, production, finance, design, administration and management, for example, when two companies join together, there is only need for one marketing department. Alternatively, integration can be viewed as a means of gaining greater control of the market for the company concerned, through greater market share, e.g. Guinness and Grand Metropolitan. There are two types of integration that can benefit a company:

Horizontal

The joining of two companies that are in the same industry and involved in the same stage of production. For example, Lloyds and the Cheltenham and Gloucester Building Society. Both these companies benefited because the combined company had a greater market share.

Vertical

Two firms joining together involved in the same industry, but at different stages of production. For example, Thomson Holidays joining with Britannia Airways. This allows Thomson to have greater control of the dates and times of flights. Vertical integration can either be **backwards** or **forwards**. A manufacturer joining with one of its suppliers would be seen as backward vertical integration because the manufacturer had merged with a company at an earlier stage of production. This would allow the manufacturer to determine when and how the supplies required are delivered. A manufacturing company merging with a retailer would be an example of forward vertical integration. This provides the manufacturer with a guaranteed market for the goods produced.

There are some cases where the two companies merging do so to gain the benefits of diversification, and therefore spreading the risks by having an involvement in a range of businesses. This is called **conglomerate** integration, a good example of which is British American Tobacco, whose product portfolio comprises of cigarettes, toilet basins and financial services to name but a few! However, companies may view integration in a different way, for example, Unilever, selling fast moving consumer goods (FMCGs) in a world market, requires an integrated approach within the company. All parts of the business have to be able to work together to enable it to function effectively and compete with world-class competitors such as Proctor and Gamble, L'Oreal and Nestle.

Unilever – an integrated company

Unilever is an excellent example of a company which must be integrated in all aspects of its operations. The company is half British owned and half Dutch owned and employs over 300,000 people worldwide. It operates in 150 countries, spanning five continents, with its products being sold in a further 70 countries through local retailers. At least 1000 brands are sold, mainly in the fast moving consumer goods (FMCG) sector. The data below illustrates the size of such a company.

Many of Unilever's brands are market leaders, which normally means achieving the highest market share. Its success has been built upon the quality, reliability, efficiency and safety of its products and a close relationship with the immediate customer (retailer or industrial client), as well as its final customer: the consumer.

In an attempt to maintain its competitive advantage,

the company must invest in Research and Development (R and D) for the innovation and

	Europe	North America	Africa Middle East Latin America Asia & Pacific	Global
Ice cream	●	●	●	●
Tea based beverages	●	●	●	●
Margarine	●	●	●	●
Meal sauces	●			
Dressings	●			
Frozen foods	●			
Fabric cleaning			●	
Personal wash	●	●	●	●
Prestige fragrances			●	●
Deodorants		●		●
Hair care			●	
Mass skin care		●	●	

(Number one position)

Unilever's leadership in key product areas

improvement of its vast product range. In addition, the company relies upon creative, imaginative advertising to differentiate its products from those of its competitors, but also to ensure a unique image for each of its own brands. The list on page 130 shows the many brands of Unilever which you will have heard of, but perhaps not have associated with the name Unilever.

For Year Ending 31/12/98

Sales revenue	£27.1 billion
Operating profit	£3.0 billion
Research and development	£556 million
Advertising and promotion	£3.5 billion
Capital investment (factories/machinery)	£890 million

Source: Annual Accounts 1998, Unilever

Product	Brand
Margarine	Blue Band, Flora
Tea	Brooke Bond PG Tips
Ice cream	Cornetto, Carte d'Or
Culinary products	Bachelor's Chicken Tonight, Oxo
Frozen foods and bakery products	Birds Eye
Fabric cleaning	Persil, Surf, Radion
Personal wash	Lux, Dove, Lifebuoy
Household cleaning	Jif, Domestos
Personal fragrances	Calvin Klein products
Deodorants	Lynx, Brut, Impulse
Hair care	Sunsilk, Timotei
Skincare	Vaseline
Oral care	Signal, Mentadent, SR

Due to its global presence, Unilever has to compete with both local and international companies. According to the company's Chief Executive, Niall FitzGerald, the company aims to be 'multi-local, multi-national', i.e. it must satisfy requirements at all levels of its operations. This requires detailed knowledge and understanding of the multiplicity of markets and requires close communication between marketing, production and design teams across the world. This is in order to ensure that a consistent, targeted advertising campaign sells products which are made and designed according to specific local customer requirements. Any inconsistency in the messages which the company conveys to its markets could mean lost customers, and therefore lost revenue and profit.

Unilever – an integrated organization

The following is a quotation from one of Unilever's company brochures.

> "The challenges are choice and priority – how best to allocate our resources and shape our portfolio. To do this we need an organization that distinguishes clearly between corporate strategic leadership and operational execution."

In an attempt to achieve this, Unilever introduced changes to the organization in March 1996. The new organization is an attempt to be effective in meeting the needs of the future (see figure below), whilst recognizing the constraints of managing such a large company.

There is a strong regional focus to enable decisions to be made by those that know the local market and their products.

● An executive committee (with representatives from each of the named categories) is responsible

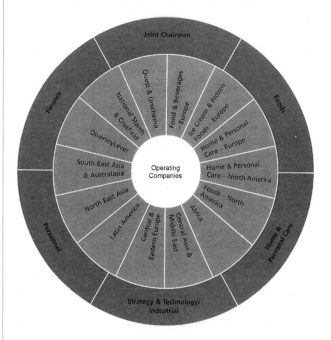

Unilever – the organization
Source: *Shaping for Outstanding Performance*, Unilever, 1996

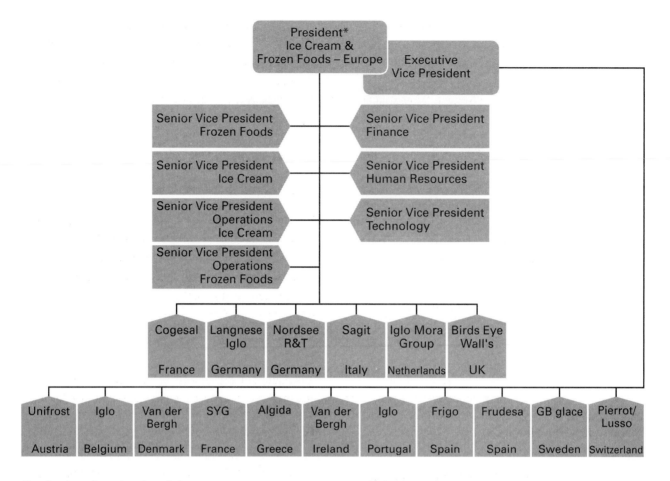

Product and region breakdown

for making decisions that affect the company as a whole, providing leadership and a directional overview for all the individual companies around the world that are part of Unilever.

- The next layer within the organizational structure provides the management for the actual operation of the member companies of Unilever. This layer is divided into the various business groups such as Ice cream and Frozen Foods, and Food and Beverages – Europe. It is important to note that these groups are based on both categories of products, e.g. Home and Personal Care, Food and Beverage, and regions around the world, e.g. Europe, Africa, Latin America (see figure above).
- The third layer consists of the individual companies within the specific group and the different countries within that particular region of the world, e.g. Birds Eye Wall's UK.

CASE STUDY

Integration across the world – Magnum ice cream

Since its launch in 1989, Magnum has developed to become a billion dollar brand. It is as successful in Sweden, Thailand and the United Arab Emirates as it is in Britain. All this from the unlikely starting point of a children's brand called Nogger.

It was Wall's sister company in Germany, Langnese-Iglo, that decided to try a larger, better quality version of their chocolate-covered ice cream for children and to call it Magnum Nogger. Research showed that adults were the most enthusiastic about the product, though they rejected the children's image suggested by the name Nogger. 'Magnum' was born.

Once the target consumer was identified as adults, further development led to a thick coating of high quality chocolate, dairy ice cream and a distinctive foil wrapping. Magnum was an immediate success when launched in Germany, Belgium, Denmark, Holland, Sweden and Switzerland in 1989. In its first year it sold four times the forecast sales volume.

Year	Volume share %
1995	16.7
1996	16.2
1997	17.0
1998	15.4

Magnum share of total wrapped impulse market (***volume***)

'Ich und mein Magnum'

Successful though the launch was, there was much to be learned still about the product and its consumers. Market research revealed that Magnum purchasers felt unusually intensely about the brand. According to Jean Callanan, international brand manager for Magnum: 'This brand has really got under the consumer's skin. People talk very passionately about it, across many countries.' Hence the advertising campaign 'Me & My Magnum', which has been successful throughout the world.

Klaus Rabbel, chairman of the Magnum International Brand Group, stresses that the success lies not in advertising alone, but in the entire marketing mix, including its 'wonderful product quality; global name, size and generosity; packaging and price'. In other words the input from designers, production teams and quality controllers is as important as that from the marketing executives.

This point can and should be taken further. For an ice cream to be successful, sophisticated distribution and production systems are vital. A week of good weather places enormous strains upon the supply chain, as demand can easily treble. So the 19 factories worldwide that produce Magnums have to be capable of rapid acceleration in their rate of production. No less importantly, the distribution system must be capable of rushing extra products to retailers throughout the world.

Ten years ago, a heatwave would empty the ice cream cabinets of Britain, leaving them empty for days. Now Wall's promises all its retailers to deliver their orders within a day, no matter how great the demand. This has only become possible through heavy investment in equipment and information technology. Here, as with every other aspect of the Magnum story, the heavy investment costs were always available from the parent company, Unilever. Without the financial strength, nothing else would have been possible.

So Magnum is a success story based upon good financial, marketing, production and design management. The future of the brand rests with an International Brand Group that has to coordinate and integrate the work of staff in 19 factories and 38 countries worldwide. It must also foster the work of the International Development Unit for Magnum, in Germany, which has been responsible for successful new variants such as Almond and Mint. Other product developments from the German team have included Walnut, Cappuccino and Coffee. These have not been introduced to Britain but are strong sellers in other countries.

Magnum is a rising star for Unilever and looks set to remain one for many years to come. In 1996, for example, all four Magnum flavours were in the UK's top ten best-selling impulse ice creams. Managing its rapid growth, coordinating the work of many thousands of staff worldwide and – above all – maintaining or enhancing the brand image is the task of executives such as Jean Callanan and Klaus Rabbel. To have taken a product for German children to millions of adult customers worldwide has been an extraordinary achievement of the brand's first six years. The next six years look likely to be just as exciting. Magnum in Tokyo? Magnum in China?

What about Brazil?

Although Unilever is a world leader in the ice cream market, there are geographic variations in its market position and in ice cream consumption (see graph below). In the USA, for instance, annual consumption per capita is 20 litres, compared with 8 litres in Europe.

In October 1997, Unilever acquired Kibon, Brazil's leading ice cream company for US$ 930 million. Brazil's 160 million consumers eat on average just over one litre of ice cream each year, so the challenge for Unilever is to develop Kibon's potential by applying Unilever's world-wide expertise in ice cream manufacturing and marketing. In addition to introducing innovative new products, manufacturing costs could be reduced and product availability could be increased.

Kibon will also be part of Unilever's new regional strategy (see section on 'Unilever – an integrated organisation', page 130). The market for ice cream in

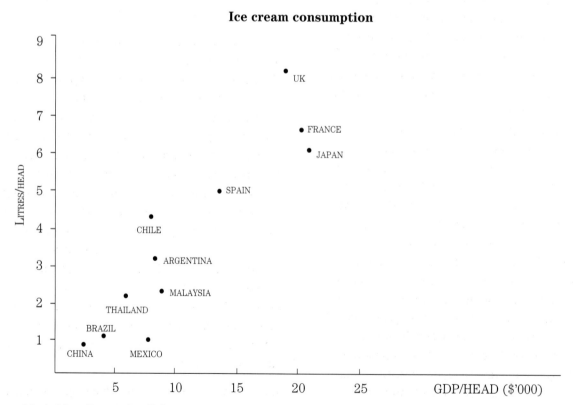

Ice cream consumption

Source: Adapted from Euromonitor, Unilever

Latin America is huge and Kibon will provide a focus for expertise in innovation, marketing, branding, sales and distribution which can be applied to Unilever's other 10 ice cream businesses in the region.

Globalization: no longer worlds apart

Globalization is the process by which companies are seeking to expand their operations to achieve greater market participation. In its simplest form, this means companies are attempting to increase sales and profits by finding new markets and different locations across the globe. Such a situation has evolved over many years, the following factors making a significant contribution to the process.

- The growing integration of the world economy has seen a decline in the costs of transport and communication. Between 1930 and 1990, average revenue per mile in air transport fell from 68 US cents to 11 cents, in 1990 value. The cost of a three-minute telephone call between New York and London fell from $244.65 to $3.32. Between 1960 and 1990, the cost of a unit of computing power fell 99 per cent.
- Technological change has made globalization easier by allowing communication between people on either side of the globe. Electronic mail and the Internet have contributed a great deal to this. Stock markets and banks are linked by computers and, therefore, it is easier to transfer money across frontiers than ever before.
- Fear of fluctuations in exchange rates has encouraged the spread of production capacity across frontiers, so that many companies have deliberately moved operations to guard against the uncertainty of changing exchange rates.
- Barriers to trade, e.g. import taxes (customs duties) and quotas, have been greatly reduced, mainly due to the work of the World Trade Organization, using GATT (General Agreement on Trade and Tariffs) as the vehicle for change. It is estimated, for example, that the average tariff by 1990 stood at about 7 per cent, representing an 80 per cent reduction since the 1950s.
- Governments have realized that by reducing their protection of local industries and inviting foreign investment, jobs are created and with them, economic prosperity. As a result of this, a range of new markets – notably in Asia and Eastern Europe – have opened to foreign investment.

The definition of globalization differs from industry to industry. The problem comes when a company mass-produces its products in a single location, but sells to a world-wide market. Differences in cultures and consumer expectations mean that companies must be aware of such differences and respond accordingly with product variations. Globalization to Boeing means a single production process and widespread marketing and distribution – that is why there are no local manufacturers of Jumbo jets. To Holiday Inn, the international brand is successful because of customers who need to stay in a hotel with an international brand name in unfamiliar environments – this is why the local, small hotels carrying Holiday Inn's brand name are successful.

In recent years there has been a shift in the reasons why companies move production overseas. Historically, companies have located production abroad in order to overcome natural or artificial barriers to trade, e.g. poor access to raw materials, or excessive import taxes. Alternatively, the need for the cheapest labour drove companies to locate in certain areas. If producing at the lowest cost was the **only** criterion, it would have made sense for many companies to locate all their production at a single base, in order to exploit economies of scale. In practice, however, governments in consuming countries have pushed companies to spread production more widely. For example, much of the Japanese investment in the US and the European Union was a response to protection against its exports, by reducing the number of products which could be imported.

Many of these trends are now changing. Reduction of trade barriers now makes traditional protectionjumping production unnecessary. Improvements in communications are eliminating natural barriers to long-distance commerce; services can now be produced in one country and exported to another, just like manufactured goods. In Europe, at least, Economic and Monetary Union (EMU) will eliminate exchange rate fluctuations. Therefore, creating overseas production sites, merely to meet local consumption, looks an increasingly fragile basis for foreign investment. A much better reason is the ability to make the best use of a company's competitive advantages by locating production wherever it is most efficient. Today's multi-nationals create widespread networks of research, component production, assembly and distribution.

PROBLEMS?

When companies look for the cheapest source of materials, they may attract unnecessary attention from the media, e.g. Nike, the sports shoe group. On paper, its strategy of subcontracting the production of its shoes to local factories looks eminently sensible. But these arrangements have turned into a public relations nightmare in recent years, as campaigners have complained of 'sweatshop' conditions in many of the Asian plants.

Financial markets across the world have become so closely linked that a significant change in one stock market or exchange rate can have severe effects on the opposite side of the globe. The recent turmoil in the Hong Kong SE resulted in a crash in the FTSE100, although British investors only hold about 7 per cent of their money in Far-Eastern companies. The collapse of the Yamaichi bank (Japan's fourth largest bank) in November 1997, also sent shock waves around the world, resulting in various stock market crashes. The benefits of easy access to capital can be far outweighed by the repercussions.

CASE STUDY

Ford and Honda: each in their own way

Rising costs and the world-wide spread of shared tastes in car styling have prompted the industry's giants to exploit global economies of scale, although in different ways.

Ford traditionally operated on a regional basis, with a large degree of power delegated from its US headquarters. Products, therefore, differed sharply depending on local executives' points of view on consumer tastes. Honda, by contrast, is a much younger company which grew rapidly from making motor cycles in the 1950s. In contrast to Ford, Honda was run very firmly from Japan. Until well into the 1980s, its vehicles were designed, engineered and built in Japan for sale around the world.

Significantly, however, Honda tended to be more flexible than Ford in developing new products. Rather than having a structure based on independent functional departments, such as bodywork or engines, all Japan's car manufacturers preferred multi-disciplinary teams taken from a range of company activities, e.g. marketing, production, personnel.

In 1993, Alex Trotman, Ford's newly-appointed chairman, created 'Ford 2000', replacing functional departments with multi-disciplinary product teams which allowed greater responsiveness to change. Honda decentralized by giving cars the same name, but with different versions according to the needs of local markets. Honda's engineers have designed the car to have common basic structural parts, known as standardization, e.g. chassis, doors, roofs, but the variations lie in the products' features. The teams were based on five (now three) vehicle centres, which were responsible for different types of car models. Small and medium-sized cars, for example, are handled by a European team split between the UK and Germany. Each takes charge of one area of the process, whether technical, financial or marketing-based. While Honda's cars have much the same names around the world, they are becoming less, rather than more, standardized. 'Globalization' – a global strategy with local management – is the watchword. Honda engineers also reckon they can now devise basic engineering structures which are common enough to allow significant economies of scale, but sufficiently flexible to be altered to suit regional variations.

 DISCUSSION POINTS

1 If a company wishes to consider expanding into Africa, what information should the company obtain before taking such a decision? Hint – the following areas may be worthy of consideration: marketing, production, finance, location, communication, human resource management, costs, revenues.

2 What kind of problems would a company like Unilever face on a day-to-day basis because of the fact that it operates in over 200 countries worldwide?

Source: *Financial Times*, 1997

ACTIVITY

Time for tea

In the UK, while tea is still the most popular drink, tea manufacturers are concerned that the percentage of the population drinking tea on a daily basis is starting to decline as the chart below shows. The only sectors of the beverage market showing growth over the last 5 years are soft drinks and alcohol.

Percentage of population over 10 years old drinking daily

	1992	1993	1994	1995	1996
Tea	78.7	78.1	77.1	77.0	76.2
Coffee	56.9	57.2	55.9	53.7	54.4
Alcohol	29.7	29.7	25.9	31.8	32.8
Soft drinks	53.7	53.5	55.7	57.7	57.1

Source: National drinks survey

Tea manufacturers are looking for ways to boost tea consumption, particularly among young people. They have tried various innovations in recent years and more are in the pipeline.

Research each of the following. Identify their product attributes and assess their relative success to date and likely chances of success in the future, within the context of the UK beverages market.

1 Instant tea-granules

2 Round tea-bags

3 Pyramid tea-bags

4 Iced tea

5 Ready-to-drink hot tea in cans

6 Tea shops

7 Health aspects of tea

Index